"Darrow Miller and his colleagues strip away the ideological baggage that the term 'social justice' has acquired over time to reveal its heart: compassion that is firmly rooted in a biblical worldview. Their invitation to the church to embrace it as a key component of its mission is a clarion call that must not and cannot be ignored. This book must be required reading for every discerning Christian around the world who seeks to understand the crux of the biblical command to love one's neighbor."

ABRAHAM GEORGE, director,
International Church Mobilization, International Justice Mission (IJM)

"No one explains Christian principles of poverty-fighting more clearly than Darrow Miller. His latest book, *Rethinking Social Justice*, should be required reading at Christian colleges. No one offers challenges better-grounded in reality and more deeply based on the understanding that 'Christ did not die to make us safe.' If you have bought into either Social Universalism or Social Darwinism, the two left and right definitions of social justice, this book will challenge you to re-think and then re-act."

MARVIN OLASKY, editor in chief, World News Group

"In his new book *Rethinking Social Justice: Restoring Biblical Compassion*, Darrow Miller does not try to redefine 'social justice.' Instead he answers the question, 'How can we best ensure that justice supports flourishing for everyone in every area of life—economic, political, social, and so forth?' He shows us, as Christians, how to practice what we preach and 'to do justice, and to love kindness, and to walk humbly with our God' from both a biblical and a real-world perspective. This is the book that I have been waiting for on justice, a must-read for all Christians."

HUGH WHELCHEL, executive director,
The Institute for Faith, Work and Economics

"In an era where the doing of 'justice' is more and more popular, the challenge for the church is now less about the activity of doing social justice and more about doing it well and doing it in the name of Jesus. *Rethinking Social Justice* is an important addition to the conversation about the effective definition and practice of social justice for the church."

KEITH WRIGHT, president and CEO, Thrive Global, LLC

"Nietzsche commented sarcastically that if he was to believe in Jesus as Redeemer, Christians are going to have to look more redeemed. Certainly in our world of ecological, social, and economic injustice, that will mean the church must be a compassionate community seeking justice. But sadly, humanists sometimes have been ahead of the church on this, and thus they have often defined the terms of the debate. Yet the gospel opening up into the biblical worldview provides the true context for understanding and embodying social justice. That is what this book tries to do: ground our call to social justice in a biblical vision of the world. This is a wise book coming from authors who are grounded in Scripture and who have been practicing what they write about for decades. It will help readers to think and spur them to act more faithfully. I heartily commend this book."

MICHAEL W. GOHEEN, PhD
theological director, Missional Training Center, Phoenix,
and coauthor of *The Drama of Scripture* and *Living at the Crossroads*

"Reading Darrow Miller's *Rethinking Social Justice* takes one on a journey through the history of worldviews and ideas to see how radically justice, poverty, compassion, and gospel thinking devolved. The gospel of Jesus going about doing good and healing those under the power of the Devil transformed into a gospel of going to heaven when we die. Compassion morphs from an attitude involving helping action to a mere feeling of sorrow for another's pain. Poverty of relationship with God and neighbor, of honor and dignity becomes merely a lack of money or goods. Justice degenerates from a moral and metaphysical matter to a solely physical and economic one. Miller's careful probing builds a strong case for a full justice, economic as well as religious and spiritual, growing up from divine compassion is God's kingdom agenda."

GERRY BRESHEARS, PhD
professor of theology, Western Seminary, Portland

RETHINKING
SOCIAL
JUSTICE

BOOKS BY DARROW L. MILLER

Servanthood: The Vocation of All Christians

Discipling Nations: The Power of Truth to Transform Cultures,
with Stan Guthrie

God's Remarkable Plan for the Nations, with Scott Allen and Bob Moffitt

God's Unshakable Kingdom, with Scott Allen and Bob Moffitt

The Worldview of the Kingdom of God, with Scott Allen and Bob Moffitt

Against All Hope: Hope for Africa, with Scott Allen and the African
Working Group of Samaritan Strategy Africa

On Earth as It Is in Heaven: Making It Happen, with Bob Moffitt

The Forest in the Seed, with Scott Allen

*Nurturing the Nations: Reclaiming the Dignity of Women in Building
Healthy Cultures,* with Stan Guthrie

LifeWork: A Biblical Theology for What You Do Every Day,
with Marit Newton

*Emancipating the World: A Christian Response to Radical Islam and
Fundamentalist Atheism*

Recovering Our Mission: Making the Invisible Kingdom Visible

DARROW L. MILLER

with Scott Allen and Gary Brumbelow

Foreword by John Stonestreet

RETHINKING SOCIAL JUSTICE

Restoring Biblical Compassion

YWAM PUBLISHING

Seattle, Washington

YWAM Publishing is the publishing ministry of Youth With A Mission (YWAM), an international missionary organization of Christians from many denominations dedicated to presenting Jesus Christ to this generation. To this end, YWAM has focused its efforts in three main areas: (1) training and equipping believers for their part in fulfilling the Great Commission (Matthew 28:19), (2) personal evangelism, and (3) mercy ministry (medical and relief work).

For a free catalog of books and materials, call (425) 771-1153 or (800) 922-2143. Visit us online at www.ywampublishing.com.

Published by YWAM Publishing
a ministry of Youth With A Mission
P.O. Box 55787, Seattle, WA 98155-0787

Library of Congress Cataloging-in-Publication Data
Miller, Darrow L.
   Rethinking social justice : restoring biblical compassion / Darrow L. Miller, with Scott Allen and Gary Brumbelow.
      pages cm
   Includes bibliographical references and index.
   ISBN 978-1-57658-793-5 (pbk. : alk. paper) — ISBN 978-1-57658-884-0 (e-book : alk. paper)
   1. Social justice—Religious aspects—Christianity. 2. Social justice—Biblical teaching. I. Title.
   BR115.J8M55 2015
   261.8—dc23   2014043935

Unless otherwise noted, Scripture quotations in this book are taken from The Holy Bible: New International Version®. NIV®. Copyright © 1979, 1984, 2011 by Biblica, formerly International Bible Society. All rights reserved. Verses marked NKJV are taken from the New King James Version®. Copyright © 1982 by Thomas Nelson, Inc. Used by permission. All rights reserved. Verses marked NASB are taken from the New American Standard Bible®, Copyright © 1960, 1962, 1963, 1968, 1971, 1972, 1973, 1975, 1977, 1995 by The Lockman Foundation. Used by permission.

References to "Webster" or "Webster's 1828 Dictionary," unless otherwise noted, indicate the *American Dictionary of the English Language* by Noah Webster, 1828 facsimile ed. (San Francisco: Foundation for American Christian Education, 1967).

First printing 2015

Printed in the United States of America

CONTENTS

FOREWORD

G. K. Chesterton once said, "The Church and the heresies always used to fight about words, because they are the only thing worth fighting about."[1] He understood that definitions matter greatly. In fact, the way a word is defined can determine the direction of millions of dollars in a national budget or millions of people in a civilization.

The term *social justice* comprises two such fighting words, particularly among Christians today. Some claim the church has been too much about "hearing" and not enough about "doing." God hates injustice, they say, and thus the Christian is called to be about this thing called "social justice." In a sense, they are certainly right. The Old Testament is full of references in which God calls his people to care for the poor, immigrants, and the environment.

Other Christians smell a socialist rat in all this "justice" talk. To them, advocating for social justice seems to be little more than a call for more government redistribution and intervention, an attack on free markets and corporate profit. They accuse the other side of using scriptures as decoration for talking points from failed and dangerous ideologies. Talking heads warn, "If your church preaches social justice, run!" Or, "Jesus said the poor will always be with us. We don't need to worry about helping them in the name of the gospel."

But we cannot run from the biblical appeal to justice. Christians are to be restorers of the good, the true, and the beautiful. Darrow Miller has articulated for decades that the Great Commission must include work not only to proclaim the gospel but also to enact the gospel, demonstrating the fullness of Christ's authority over the world he created.

What, then, is to be done? First, we must clearly and biblically define what justice actually is. This is going to require defining other terms as well. For example, if we wish to alleviate poverty, we must first answer the question, what is the nature of poverty? If poverty is purely a lack of financial resources, the solution is obvious. But experience tells us that giving money to poor people doesn't always solve the problem. Clues abound that people can be relationally, morally, or culturally poor. Thus, our task is to care for the poor not only with our hearts but also with our heads.

Second, we must not truncate the gospel. The late Chuck Colson was very fond of quoting Dutch theologian and statesman Abraham Kuyper, who said, "There is not a single square inch in the whole domain of our human existence over which Jesus Christ, who is Sovereign over *all*, does not cry: 'Mine!'"[2] This means we cannot run from the call to justice. We must join in the restoring, redeeming, reconciling, regenerating work of Christ in the world. Seeking justice is surely part of this.

Third, we must act. From prison, Dietrich Bonhoeffer wrote to his former students at Finkenwalde Seminary: "Bravely take hold of the real, not dallying now with what might be. Not in the flight of ideas but only in action is freedom. Make up your mind and come out into the tempest of living."[3] This will bridge the hearing and doing. This will help close the often growing gap between younger and older generations of Christ followers. We need not—indeed we must not—choose between truth and action.

I am thrilled that the Disciple Nations Alliance has undertaken the challenge to write this book. I've recommended Darrow Miller's writing for years; he's an example of the power of marrying truth and action. He has worked across the globe and seen the power of the gospel applied in various contexts to various degrees of social brokenness. He is indubitably qualified to speak to this impasse.

A final word to my generation: we can often be grumpy about the older generation who "just didn't get it." Much of the confusion surrounding "social justice" can be chalked up to a selective memory on our part. There are great men and women, even in recent years, whom we can follow in our pursuit of truth, love, and justice.

I had the privilege of working with one of these people during the last three years of his life. Charles W. Colson was one of the greatest advocates for truth *and* for justice for "the least of these" that the church (even the world!) has ever seen. And I think Chuck would have really liked and appreciated this book. It deserves to be taken seriously.

JOHN STONESTREET
Speaker and Fellow of the
Chuck Colson Center for Christian Worldview

PREFACE

The phrase "social justice" has become quite popular within evangelical circles in the past few years. But what exactly do people mean when they use this phrase? For many, it is simply another way of saying "serving the poor." For others, it carries with it an implicit approach to poverty fighting, one defined by involuntary resource redistribution and socialist notions of equality. Indeed, many people, including many Christians, equate these ideas.

I have long been deeply concerned about issues of poverty and development. My journey among the poor began when, as a nineteen-year-old college student, I spent the summer working in an orphanage in Mexico City. My heart was broken by the plight of the poor. The things I saw and experienced not only changed my life; they set the course of my life. At the time, I remember thinking, "When I die, there needs to be less poverty in the world than there is today." Little did I know how my life would be altered.

As a young man, I was a socialist in my orientation. I assumed that the root of poverty was that the poor lacked money or resources and that the solution was simply to redistribute resources from the wealthy to the poor. Ron Sider's book *Rich Christians in an Age of Hunger*, published first in 1977, both reinforced my thinking and motivated the course of my life. Here was an evangelical Christian who had a heart for the poor. There were not many such people in the 1970s! Sider wanted to engage the evangelical community in helping to solve the plight of the poor. His solution supported my assumptions that to solve the problems of poverty we needed to redistribute resources from the rich to the poor.

Many of the readers of this book may be able to relate to both my passion and thinking. I am thankful to say that fifty years later, the passion is still there as much as it was when I was in my early twenties. But after years of engaging in the world of poverty, I have come to understand there is a

more basic problem than simply a lack of money; and thus there is a more
fundamental solution to the problem than simply redistributing resources.

I pastored for a few years in urban Denver and then spent twenty-
seven years working with an international relief and development organization, Food for the Hungry International. While at FHI, I traveled
extensively in some of the poorest countries of the world, meeting, serving, and sometimes staying with staff and the constituencies they served.

God commands us to be concerned for the plight of the poor and
needy. We are to be generous, openhanded, and compassionate. But the
Bible also provides a framework, or a worldview, in which we must do
this work of service. This worldview takes into account the nature of God
as the creator and the source of objective reality. It is based on a biblical understanding of humans and their unique qualities and position—as
made in God's image—within creation. It is founded on God's eternal
laws, both the natural laws found in creation and the moral law summarized in the Ten Commandments. Only within this framework will the
means and methods of serving the poor be God-honoring and helpful.
The implications of and approaches to poverty fighting within a biblical
framework were also explored in my 1997 book, *Discipling Nations: The
Power of Truth to Transform Cultures*.

In 2012 the Disciple Nations Alliance was approached by John
Stonestreet, speaker and author at Summit Ministries and the Chuck Colson Center for Christian Worldview, to see if we had any material related
to the topic of social justice from the basis of a biblical worldview. John
works with young Christians around the country and observed that many
are captivated by the concept of social justice. Yet he is concerned that in
the process many are being influenced by a host of assumptions whose
origin is atheistic rather than biblical. This conversation is part of what
spurred us to write a series of blog posts on social justice at *Darrow Miller
and Friends*.[1] This book is a compilation and adaptation of those posts,
and we share it in the hope that it will help Christians think critically and
biblically about this important topic.

This book has been written with the participation of two of my Disciple Nations Alliance colleagues who love to write and who understand

the power of words to shape lives and culture. Scott Allen got the project started in his initial response to John Stonestreet. His initial post at *Darrow Miller and Friends*, "What Exactly Do You Mean by 'Social Justice'?" was so successful that we decided to expand on it. Our coworker Gary Brumbelow has applied his gifts to enhance the clarity and impact of our words.

INTRODUCTION

We live at a time of Western affluence juxtaposed with intolerable poverty. Injustice and corruption continue to grip nations, and a majority of the world's people suffer the consequences.

In a world of bounty, a world that has the capacity to produce plenty of food for all, 25,000 people die every day of starvation. A majority of these are children.

We rape our environment as if its sole reason for existence is human consumption.

Gendercide—the systematic, institutional war against women—has erased 200 million females from the world. In India alone, one million human beings are killed every year because they are female.

Women and babies are objectified to the extent that each year between 40 and 50 million babies are killed before they are born, simply because they are inconvenient.

Today, globally, an estimated 20.9 million men, women, and children are enslaved for forced labor or commercial sex. In the United States, up to 293,000 children are being sexually exploited. Over 50 percent of the women in Latin America have suffered violence at the hands of a male relative.

The world remembers the horrors of the murder of 6 million Jews by the Nazis, the 11.3 million blacks sold into slavery through the Atlantic slave trade, the 17 million sold into slavery in the Middle East, and the world has cried, "Never again!"

Yet today the injustices are as bad as or worse than those of the past. Where is the justice? Where is the compassion?

It is fair to say that a world without Christ is a world without compassion. Without a good God, there is no justice. This book has been written to reclaim the biblical concept of compassion, known today more popularly as social justice.

It is vital to be clear about what we mean when we speak of "social justice." The term has political, economic, and theological implications. Social entrepreneur and pastor Ken Wytsma says,

> When we use the phrase social justice . . . it is important to note that we are not committing to the particular goals of any single political party, economic theory, or theological stance. More accurately, we are seeking to understand how the Bible's clear call to be in right relationship with both God and our fellow humans is best accomplished in our society. Perhaps the definition can be even simpler. "Social Justice" describes the elements of a just society.[1]

While there is much to affirm in this observation, the writer fails to deal with the fact that today the term "social justice" is indeed being used by proponents of Marxist economic and political theory to describe their movement. And these proponents have largely defined the popular understanding of the term in the broader culture. Pretending otherwise is a failure to take ideas seriously. Social justice is loaded with ideological baggage, whether we like it or not. We need to recognize this, examine the roots of this redefinition as well as how the term is currently used, and then define the term biblically.

In recent years the term "social justice" has been evacuated of its biblical understanding and redefined by the atheistic paradigm of modern society. Such redefinition has stripped from millions of citizens the responsibility to be compassionate and seek justice, and has instead invested that responsibility in large government bureaucracies. But by giving aid or welfare, large institutions have actually created greater dependency and poverty. This is the inevitable result of abandoning the biblical framework, the creation order that established personal responsibility, lifted people and nations out of poverty, and created a culture of justice to replace the (almost universal) culture of corruption.

When I was in college, I read Dr. Karl Menninger's book *Whatever Became of Sin?* Menninger, one of the world's leading psychiatrists and founder of the world-famous Menninger Clinic, wrote the book because he had become convinced that mental health was connected to moral health. He pointed out that the word *sin* was disappearing from the American vocabulary. With the loss of the word came the loss of the concept of real moral guilt.

At the founding of the United States, theology was the language of discourse. Americans affirmed the Creator. They lived in a moral universe in which human beings are separated from God by sin. They recognized, implicitly if not expressly, that this broken relationship leads to all sorts of brokenness within each individual, among humans, and between human beings and the rest of creation. The concept of sinfulness influenced society's understanding of human health in every dimension—moral, psychological, physical, social, and economic.

With the Western shift from a biblical to an atheistic worldview, we have lost the concepts of a moral universe, moral health, and sin. For Menninger, to lose the concept of sin was to lose the potential of restored relationships and renewed health.

Tragically, Menninger's call did not reinstate the concept of sin in society. Even more tragically, too often the church itself has abandoned the concept of sin and the accompanying biblical notion of repentance. As a culture's worldview shifts, so too does its language and life. Instead of a theological language of discourse, atheistic materialism has produced a culture whose language is psychological. Sin and shame (i.e., moral guilt) have vanished. Now we speak the language of self-esteem, of feeling good about oneself regardless of one's behavior and actions. We are no longer sinners; we are sick. We do not take responsibility for our lives but rather expect others—parents, friends, the government—to be responsible for us. Repentance and confession do not cure what ails us; we look to therapy to cure and drugs to kill the pain.

The title of Menninger's book evokes a parallel question: Whatever became of compassion? As a service to those Christians who are interested in the twin activities of reflection and action, we offer this book in two parts.

In part 1, "The Foundations and Demise of Social Justice," we deal with the definition and derivation of the terms (chap. 1) as well as some of the differences of opinion about social justice (chap. 2). From there we show how the concept of compassion has been replaced with pity (chap. 3), especially through the effects of atheism in Western societies (chap. 4). In part 2, "Redefining Social Justice in Terms of Compassion," we examine what the Bible teaches about compassion (chap. 5) before exploring seven fundamental principles of compassion (chap. 6). Finally, we tell some stories of biblical compassion in action (chap. 7) and look at Pope Francis's perspective on social justice (chap. 8).

This book was written for all who have a heart for people in poverty and who want to understand biblical insights and grow in obedience. But I have especially written for a younger generation of Christians who intuitively understand that, of all people, Christ followers should be working the hardest for social justice. You may have watched your parents' generation focus on evangelism and church planting to the exclusion of a comprehensive gospel of the kingdom. You may have grieved to see your elders largely forget that Christians are responsible to minister to people who are poor and disenfranchised.

I grieve with you. At the same time, I'm concerned. I fear that many of your generation, in reaction to this deficit in the church and in a quest to restore balance, have unknowingly embraced a false view of compassion and social justice, a perspective unknowingly derived from the modern paradigm of the Western world.

If you have a heart for the poor and are concerned about the issue of social justice, I believe you will find this book helpful.

STUDY GUIDE   *Before reading further, please turn to the Study Guide on page 157.*
SESSION 1

PART I

THE FOUNDATIONS AND DEMISE OF SOCIAL JUSTICE

CHAPTER I

WHAT IS SOCIAL JUSTICE?

Many young Christians care about social justice. They believe Christ followers should be concerned with the poor, with the care of creation, and with other political, economic, and social issues. In the Bible they see God calling his people to feed the poor, clothe the naked, shelter the homeless, and seek justice in the public square and the marketplace.

STUDY GUIDE
SESSION 2

Admonitions in both testaments provide the motivation and the context for our engagement with social justice. Here are some examples from the Old Testament:

> This is what the LORD Almighty said: "Administer true justice; show mercy and compassion to one another. Do not oppress the widow or the fatherless, the foreigner or the poor. Do not plot evil against each other." (Zech. 7:9–10)

> Learn to do right; seek justice. Defend the oppressed. Take up the cause of the fatherless; plead the case of the widow. (Isa. 1:17)

> Defend the weak and the fatherless; uphold the cause of the poor and the oppressed. (Ps. 82:3)

> He has shown you, O mortal, what is good. And what does the LORD require of you? To act justly and to love mercy and to walk humbly with your God. (Mic. 6:8)

Similarly, the New Testament makes social justice a major thrust of the expansion of the kingdom of God. Jesus calls us to love our neighbor as we love ourselves.

"Love the Lord your God with all your heart and with all your soul and with all your mind." This is the first and greatest commandment. And the second is like it: "Love your neighbor as yourself." (Matt. 22:37–39)

Jesus also reminds us that when he returns, he will sit on his throne and separate the sheep from the goats based on how we treated those in need.

When the Son of Man comes in his glory, and all the angels with him, he will sit on his glorious throne. All the nations will be gathered before him, and he will separate the people one from another as a shepherd separates the sheep from the goats. He will put the sheep on his right and the goats on his left.

Then the King will say to those on his right, "Come, you who are blessed by my Father; take your inheritance, the kingdom prepared for you since the creation of the world. For I was hungry and you gave me something to eat, I was thirsty and you gave me something to drink, I was a stranger and you invited me in, I needed clothes and you clothed me, I was sick and you looked after me, I was in prison and you came to visit me."

Then the righteous will answer him, "Lord, when did we see you hungry and feed you, or thirsty and give you something to drink? When did we see you a stranger and invite you in, or needing clothes and clothe you? When did we see you sick or in prison and go to visit you?"

The King will reply, "Truly I tell you, whatever you did for one of the least of these brothers and sisters of mine, you did for me." (Matt. 25:31–40)

Often when I teach, I refer to this passage, asking pastors and church leaders, "Is your church a 'sheep church' or a 'goat church'?" I often get a pained response.

Likewise, the apostle Paul implores us to have the mind of Christ.

> Do nothing out of selfish ambition or vain conceit. Rather, in humility value others above yourselves, not looking to your own interests but each of you to the interests of the others. (Phil. 2:3–4)

Many young Christians read these passages and wonder how previous generations of Christians could miss something so obvious. How could their predecessors have been so consumed with "spiritual salvation" and so unconcerned for the cultural mandate and the cry "thy kingdom come"? C. S. Lewis speaks of the church's culpability:

> But it did not happen, however, without sins on our parts: for that justice and that care for the poor which (most mendaciously) the Communists advertise, we in reality ought to have brought about ages ago. But far from it: we Westerners preached Christ with our lips. With our actions we brought slavery of Mammon. We are more guilty than the infidels: for to those that know the will of God and do it not, the greater the punishment.[1]

Pastor and author Timothy Keller points out that "most people know that Jesus came to bring forgiveness and grace. Less well known is the biblical teaching that a true experience of the grace of Jesus Christ inevitably motivates a man or woman to seek justice in the world."[2] The question is not, "Should Christians engage in social justice?" It is, "How can we best ensure that justice flourishes in all areas of life—economic, political, social, and so forth?"

DEFINING THE TERM

Before we proceed, let's establish a definition. "Social justice" refers to justice in the social arena. The two words to be examined are defined in Webster's 1828 dictionary as follows:

> justice: n. [L. justitia, from justus, just.] The virtue which consists in giving to everyone what is his due; practical conformity to the laws and to principles of rectitude in the dealings of men with each other; honesty; integrity in commerce or mutual intercourse. Justice is distributive or commutative. Distributive justice belongs to magistrates or rulers, and consists in distributing to every man that right or equity which the laws and the principles of equity require; or in deciding controversies according to the laws and to principles of equity. Commutative justice consists in fair dealing in trade and mutual intercourse between man and man.

> social: a. [L. socialis, from socius, companion.] Pertaining to society; relating to men living in society, or to the public as an aggregate body; as social interests or concerns; social pleasures; social benefits; social happiness; social duties. True self-love and social [sic] are the same.

Note that in the social realm there are two dimensions of justice. One is *distributive justice*: justice granted by the government which renders equity to each citizen and equality before the law. The other is *commutative justice*: justice granted in the marketplace through free and fair exchange between people; this is "social" justice in that it deals with justice in the community, between citizens and their neighbors.

According to economist and theologian Michael Novak, "Social justice is really the capacity to organize with others to accomplish certain ends for the good of the whole community." It is "a virtue, a habit that people internalize and learn, a capacity. Its capacity has two sides: first, a capacity to organize with others to accomplish particular ends and, second, ends that are extra-familial. They're for the good of the neighborhood, or the village, or the town, or the state, or the country, or the world. . . . [Social justice is] the new order of the ages."[3]

Justice is a product of kingdom culture; it is doing what is good and right toward others as well as righting the wrongs that have been done to people. Ken Wytsma points out that we reflect God's heart when we care about social justice.

> Justice is the single best word, both inside and outside the Bible, for capturing God's purposes for the world and humanity's calling in the world. Justice is, in fact, the broadest, most consistent word the Bible uses to speak about *what ought to be*. . . . To do justice means to render to each what each is due. . . . It is based on the image of God in every person—the Imago Dei—that grants all people inalienable dignity and infinite worth.[4]

Udo Middelmann offers this helpful summary of the nature of social justice:

> Social justice is not a euphemism for socialism with its disregard for personal effort, nor coercion by a state to reach equality of outcome. Justice requires the pursuit of fairness towards people, situations and genuine possibilities. A social dimension lies in the fact that we are not alone and should bear each other's burdens, whether they are educational, emotional, financial or spiritual/intellectual. Social justice addresses issues of human rights not by governmental attribution, but owned by nature of being people in the image of God, who intended a fuller life, greater knowledge and genuine responsibility for people.[5]

HISTORY OF THE TERM

The term *social justice*, while not found in Scripture, is clearly rooted in the biblical cosmology and narrative. But where did the term itself originate?

From its inception in the Bible, the concept of social justice travels through Thomas Aquinas. Aquinas wrote of *general justice*: "Now the virtue of a good citizen is general justice, whereby a man is directed to the common good."[6] A citizen has an interest not only in his or her own welfare but also in the welfare of others.

In 1840 the Italian Jesuit scholar Luigi Taparelli D'Azeglio appropriated Aquinas's concept of general justice and coined the term *social justice*. Taparelli was writing in response to the massive changes in society brought on by the Industrial Revolution. Ryan Messmore writes of Taparelli:

> His vision of social justice, then, emphasized freedom and respect for human beings and the small institutions through which they pursue basic needs. He held that true justice can't be achieved without doing justice to our social nature and natural forms of association. Social justice entailed a social order in which government doesn't overrun or crowd out institutions of civil society such as family, church and local organizations. Rather, they are respected, protected, and allowed to flourish.[7]

In 1891 Pope Leo XIII's social encyclical, *Rerum Novarum*, built on Taparelli's argument.[8]

For Aquinas, Taparelli, and Pope Leo XIII, social justice had a very different meaning than it does for many today. The Western worldview has eroded, and as a culture's worldview changes, so does its language. For example, in the language of Judeo-Christian culture, a woman carried a *baby* in her womb. In today's atheistic paradigm, the unborn baby is a "product of conception." In the West's historic paradigm, marriage was a covenantal relationship between a man and woman, before God, for life. Today the word *marriage* is being redefined in postmodern terms to mean a temporary relationship between two consenting adults. So it is with social justice. When Europe and North America shifted from the Judeo-Christian worldview to an atheist-materialist worldview, the term's original, nobler meaning became distorted.

How this narrative unfolded is discussed later in this book. Here we simply note that the modern usage of the term *social justice* is code for statist solutions to poverty. Today social justice is more likely to be associated with Marxist and socialist zero-sum economic policies. Rather than individuals forming voluntary associations to care for needs in the community, solutions are more likely to be based on government redistribution. In fact, the Institute for Development Studies at the University of Sussex argues that redistributionist programs operated by the government for solving the problems of poverty need to be expanded to the global level.[9]

Christian generosity and compassion are not the same as government-run welfare programs. In the Bible, compassion literally means "to suffer together with another." It is perfectly demonstrated by Christ, who came to suffer together with us and ultimately die on the cross on our behalf. Compassion is also demonstrated in the parable of the good Samaritan, who didn't just transfer money to help a wounded man but got his hands dirty and suffered together with him. By its very nature, compassion cannot be done from a distance. Government bureaucrats who are physically removed from needy people cannot exercise compassion, and yet for many this is what social justice implies.

EQUALITY VERSUS EQUITY

STUDY GUIDE
SESSION 3

Finally, for some the goal of social justice is for people to be equal. What does this mean, and what does it entail?

Consider these powerful words from the US Declaration of Independence, words that have become the ideological cornerstone of American civilization: "We hold these truths to be self-evident, that all men are created equal, that they are endowed by their Creator with certain unalienable Rights, that among these are Life, Liberty and the pursuit of Happiness."

First, note that the Declaration affirms all humans to be equal, *not in that we are the same*, but in that we are created by God and all bear his image. Whether young or old, male or female, black or white, rich or poor, healthy or infirm, to be human is to be made in the image of God. This fact establishes that before God and before others, each person has dignity and honor and deserves respect from neighbors and society. Being made in the image of God, each person has certain rights granted by God, "unalienable" rights that cannot be conferred or taken away by the state or any human being or institution. These rights include life, liberty, and the pursuit of happiness, the state of living within the framework of the creation laws established at the formation of the world.

However, while human beings are equal in dignity and worth, we are not born the same. Human beings are equal and unique at the same time. The law of *individuality* makes every human unique. Among billions of snowflakes, no two are alike. So also, no two human beings are alike. Even identical twins are not truly identical. Some people were made to play basketball; others can hardly dribble. Some were born to sing opera; some should sing only in the shower. People are different sizes and colors, and we are each gifted with various talents and passions. From a myriad of possibilities, each person is made to be one of a kind. God loves diversity.

Equality and *equity* are very different, though these words are often used interchangeably. Equity assumes the unique individuality of each person. While people are different, they are to be treated equally before the law; they are to be treated fairly. The uniqueness or diversity of people is a cause for celebration, not discrimination. Equity means equal rights, responsibilities, and standing before the law for all citizens. In free societies, the goal is equity among diverse peoples.

Equality, by contrast, assumes sameness, uniformity, interchangeability. Some advocate for an equal starting place, a level playing field for every citizen. Others argue for equal outcomes—that everyone has the same results in the end. The uniqueness of individuals is often undervalued. The goal of equality is to make diverse people all the same.

It's easy to see the absurdity of this philosophy. Equality means that anyone who wants to be on the starting lineup of the Los Angeles Lakers should be allowed to play! And at the end of the season, every team in the league should have the same win-loss record.

Equality, pushed to its natural conclusion, would divide an insulin dose equally between a healthy child and a diabetic child. Equity, on the other hand, gives the diabetic child all the insulin.

Whereas equality seeks numerically equal outcomes for all people, equity seeks impartiality for diverse people. Because people are born unique, there will always be diverse starting places and outcomes. The only alternative to this is tyranny. In *The Screwtape Letters* C. S. Lewis imagines a demon instructing another demon:

> The moral is plain. Allow no preeminence among your subjects. Let no man live who is wiser or better or more famous or even handsomer than the mass. Cut them all down to a level: all slaves, all ciphers, and all nobodies. All equals.[10]

This was the goal of the communist experiments in the Soviet Union and China and the direction of all utopian experiments. People were to dress the same, act the same, and think the same under penalty of death for any deviation.

Regarding all humans as equal before the law leads to freedom, while forcing a material equality of outcome promotes tyranny. Social justice as God intended seeks equity, not equality, for a nation's citizens.

CHAPTER 2

PARADIGMS OF
SOCIAL JUSTICE

A ll people of goodwill—those who have a heart for the poor and vulnerable, who are appalled by the corruption and injustice they see,
who are aghast at the slaughter of females in modern China on the scale
of another holocaust, who grieve to watch sex slavery replace black slavery—want to do something to stand for justice.

But how do we work for social justice? What policies and programs
are needed? This is hotly debated. The heat is actually generated, though,
at a level much deeper than policies and programs.

Policies, and the programs derived from them, are not suspended in
midair; they are the logical consequences of paradigms and the principles
which flow from those paradigms. People with a heart for social justice
often hold to differing paradigms or worldviews. These sacred belief systems ultimately determine how we understand the issues surrounding
social justice and how those issues are to be solved. Different paradigms
establish very different policies and programs. Discussions of social justice may occur at the level of policies and programs, but the people in the
discussions get hot under the collar because their paradigms, which they
may hold subconsciously, are being challenged.

The following "Four P" diagram shows how paradigms drive principles, which drive policies, which drive programs.

PARADIGMS → PRINCIPLES → POLICIES → PROGRAMS

To put it differently, politics and economics are downstream from culture, and culture is downstream from "cult," another word for worship. Worldviews lead to values, which shape behaviors, which drive consequences.

The way a person defines a problem will determine how he or she solves it. Many people are motivated by compassion to help the poor. They have a worthy goal of reducing or ending poverty and injustice. But different paradigms will lead to very different solutions.

Wherever we can, we need to work together. Yet at the same time we must avoid minimizing real differences in our approach to solving problems of poverty. We need to be respectful when we speak about, and engage, others who are working with the poor, even when we disagree about how best to solve the problems our communities and nations face.

Most people who speak of social justice do so because they believe the universe has a moral dimension. That is to say, there is evil in the universe, and it manifests itself in three distinct forms: moral, natural, and institutional. Those who seek justice have the responsibility to fight evil in all its manifestations, to do what is right and oppose what is wrong. Because the universe is moral, we have a responsibility to relate ethically and justly to other human beings and to the creation. We *are* our brother's keeper! We have a responsibility to steward the creation. We are responsible for ourselves, our families, and the larger community, including people who are economically and politically marginalized.

To seek justice in a fallen world is not easy, as Dietrich Bonhoeffer's story so powerfully illustrates. As darkness grew in Europe during the rise of the Third Reich, young Pastor Bonhoeffer recognized that the church needed to stand against the injustice being perpetrated against the Jews. He challenged the church to engage on three levels, each more difficult and dangerous than the last.

First, he called the church to *advocacy*—to speak out on behalf of Jewish people. Second, he called the church to *compassion*—to come alongside Jewish neighbors in passion and suffer with them, opening their communities and homes to shelter and hide those who were being persecuted. The lives of Corrie ten Boom and the gentiles who hid Anne Frank, her family, and other Jews, are testimonies of the price paid by those who provided safety for the Jews. Third, Bonhoeffer called the church to live out *justice*—in this case, to throw a wrench in the Nazi killing machine. He called the church to stand against the unjust legal authority and to do everything possible to stop it. For Bonhoeffer, who was a confirmed pacifist, it meant taking the radical step of joining the Valkyrie plot to assassinate Hitler.

As each level of engagement increased in difficulty, more and more Christians abandoned the cry for justice. Bonhoeffer ended up paying with his life.

THE UNIVERSE, ECONOMICS, AND MORALITY

STUDY GUIDE
SESSION 4

Two dimensions of belief drive our view and practice of compassion. First, either the universe is open to intervention or it is closed. Second, either the universe has an objective moral code or it does not. Because God exists, the universe is open to transcendent intervention and it is a moral universe. If God does not exist, as argued by atheists, materialists, and others, then nature is all that is real and the universe is a "closed system" without morals. An amoral, closed system will inevitably lead to a particular economic system that can best be described by the social evolutionist concept of survival of the fittest.

Open system vs. closed system

The first dimension in our paradigm of the universe—whether we believe in an open or closed system—will determine how we define social justice, what policies we establish, and which programs we implement. The following table indicates how our paradigms drive very different principles regarding social justice.

	JUDEO-CHRISTIAN THEISM	ATHEISTIC MATERIALISM
THE UNIVERSE	Open system	Closed system
HUMAN BEINGS	The image of God	Mouths to feed
RESOURCES	Product of human imagination	Physical things in the ground
ECONOMICS	Positive sum	Zero sum
NATURE OF EQUALITY	Equal before the law	Equal outcomes
SOLVING POVERTY	Create wealth	Redistribute scarce resources
GOVERNMENT	Internal self-government; the state is responsible to its free citizens	The state must be large enough to force its will on the people
PROPERTY	Private	Belongs to the state
SOCIAL JUSTICE	Personal and public flourishing	Material equality
OPERATING PRINCIPLE	Freedom	Tyranny
POOR PEOPLE	Individuals in the community	A class only a large government can help

The Bible presents the cosmos as an *open system*. The God of the universe stands outside creation, and the system is open to intervention and the Creator's involvement. The universe is also open to the activity of angels and of human beings, those created in God's image. A *closed system* is the view of atheists, who assume that there is no God, that matter is all there is, and that no supernatural beings, neither God nor angels, exist to intervene in the system of material cause and effect. Human beings are products of purposeless evolution, cogs in the machine of the universe.

People who recognize that the universe is open understand that resources are the product of human imagination and creativity. Wealth may be created. Think of the wealth and jobs created by Apple. Steve Jobs and Steve Wozniak founded Apple in April 1976. In April 2012 Apple's value reached $600 billion, greater than the GDP of all but about eighteen of the world's countries. Apple has created more than 500,000 jobs in the United States alone. All this came from the minds of two men created in God's image.

The problems of hunger, poverty, and injustice cannot be solved without fostering a social, economic, and political environment of freedom where people and communities may flourish by creating and stewarding wealth in all its forms. This leads to a *positive-sum* economic system. In such a system, social justice focuses on personal and public flourishing in all areas of life. People are treated as free and responsible moral agents who are to practice internal self-government, allowing for limited external (national) government.

People who believe the universe is closed think that resources are physical things "in the ground" (or in the sea or the air) that are, by nature, limited. Human beings are the product of an evolutionary process, merely animals with mouths and stomachs. More people equal more mouths to feed. In a world of scarce resources, the way to solve poverty is to reduce the number of mouths or redistribute the resources, or both. A closed view of the universe establishes a *zero-sum* economic system. In such a system, social justice is defined as equal outcomes. Only a large government with authority and power to redistribute scarce resources can achieve equal outcomes and thus "social justice."

This perspective reduces social justice to a focus on the narrow realm of material poverty. Poor individuals are not seen as neighbors to be given care and opportunity. Rather, they are treated as a class that is encouraged to see government programs as the solution and for whom "docking mechanisms"[1] with such programs are created. This leads to dependency and greater poverty. Thus, we end up with a modern institution of economic and political slavery in which the well-intentioned political class gains power and influence over a compliant poor class, the newly dependent slaves.

Moral universe vs. amoral universe

What we have just described are the two distinct frameworks—open system versus closed system—for a response to the imperative to work

toward social justice. These two different views of the universe drive two
very different concepts of economics and their corresponding philosophies and practices of compassion. The other dimension of belief driving our view and practice of compassion is our view of moral reality. The
Bible indicates that the universe has a moral dimension: humans are
accountable for their behavior. Atheists and materialists consciously or
subconsciously reject the idea of moral absolutes. They see the universe
as amoral. For them, there is no moral imperative to help the poor or to
seek justice in any form.

The table below combines these two dimensions. The columns capture the contrast between open-system and closed-system views, while
the rows depict the distinction between the moral and amoral views.
Those who view the universe as amoral are represented by the lower two
quadrants. People who argue for social justice occupy the top half of the
diagram. They believe that we live in a moral universe and thus have a
responsibility to seek justice. But not all who are interested in social justice acknowledge the left column, the open system of reality.

OPEN SYSTEM CLOSED SYSTEM

	OPEN SYSTEM	CLOSED SYSTEM
MORAL		
AMORAL		

Two of the quadrants in the diagram are self-consistent, and two
are inconsistent. The upper-left quadrant is consistent with the reality of
God's existence. We live in a moral universe and an open system. This is the
Bible's view of reality. Those societies where such thinking has prevailed
(i.e., nations with a heritage of Judeo-Christian thought) have flourished

as a result. The Bible comports with reality! When we live according to the intentions of the Designer, we thrive. The lower-right quadrant is also consistent, as we will see shortly.

Many people with a heart for the poor and the moral motivation to seek justice in the world function from the upper-right quadrant. But this quadrant, along with the lower-left quadrant, is inherently inconsistent. Those in the upper-right quadrant understand that the universe is moral, but they begin their reasoning from a closed-system mentality regarding resources. This is the socialist position that I held for many years as a young adult. The naturalistic thinking of Darwinian science and metaphysics, with its assumptions of limited resources, was all I knew. Those who function from a mixed framework, as I once did, want to help the poor and seek justice and even do so sacrificially. But because they consciously or subconsciously function from a closed system of limited resources, their approach to helping the poor is radically different from that of someone functioning from the theistically consistent quadrant.

The lower-left group (amoral and open) is interested not in social justice but only in self and the amassing of wealth. They live from a "memory" of an open system that explains how wealth can be created. By mixing the memory of an open system with an affirmation of an atheistic-materialistic amoral universe, they are inconsistent. They want to gain as much wealth as they can as quickly as they can without moral constraints about how to get it or use it. We may think of these folks as some corrupt version of capitalists—hedonistic, predatory, or nihilistic. But this is not capitalism in its true, original form, as envisioned by people who affirmed a moral framework for the creation and sharing of wealth.

The lower-right group (amoral and closed) functions consistently from an atheistic-materialistic perspective. The system is closed, resources are limited, and the universe has no moral constraints. People in this quadrant cynically use the term "social justice" as they create institutional dependency to accumulate political and economic power for themselves. They seek to expand the size of the state (national) government to obtain control over the masses. The result is a modern form of slavery, an economic and political plantation where the poor are enslaved in political-economic programs. In contrast to the physical slavery of the

United States before the Civil War, or the apartheid of South Africa, this is a psychological dependency: *We are poor, and there is nothing we can do about it. Our master, the omnipotent government, will secure food and shelter for us.*

If reason and moral religions are abandoned, all that is left is Nietzsche's will to power.[2] As biologist and Darwinian social philosopher Herbert Spencer (1820–1903) clearly stated, we are governed by the "survival of the fittest." Richard Dawkins, in his book *The Selfish Gene*, follows Spencer when he uses the phrase "red in tooth and claw"—from Alfred, Lord Tennyson's poem "In Memoriam A. H. H."—to describe the behavior of living things.[3] Apart from any moral foundation, reality dictates that primal power is the only law.

The modern eugenics movement was birthed out of these assumptions, as was the Nazi concept of *Lebensunwertes Leben,* or "life unworthy of life." Those considered unfit to survive and reproduce were sterilized or killed, including the physically and mentally handicapped and those considered racially inferior by the Nazi regime. Today, these same ideas underpin abortion, forced sterilization, female feticide, infanticide, euthanasia, and other population control efforts around the world.

THE TEST OF TRUTH

A key test of an idea's validity is how it plays out in actual experience—what are its results? One of the greatest challenges to the closed-system approach to social justice is this: it doesn't work. In the real world, it nearly always leads to increased injustice and poverty. Simply put, approaches to poverty fighting that are rooted in atheistic-materialistic assumptions lead to many unintended consequences. Conversely, approaches to poverty fighting that align with the true nature of creation and of humans can have powerfully positive effects.

Economic philosopher Michael Novak, in a speech titled "Don't Confuse the Common Good with Statism," discusses the lack of evidence supporting the closed-system approach to social justice:

[Some] seem to think that the way to achieve "social justice," that is, to help the poor, is to give more money to the state to distribute. . . . [They] equate social justice with turning over to the state the project of "fighting" poverty.

Where . . . is [the] evidence that this dependence on the state actually helps the poor?

The 2011 Census Report on Poverty and Income . . . displays contrary evidence. After pouring three trillion dollars (going on four trillion) during the last three years, *in the name of helping the poor and creating jobs*, the federal state's failure is breathtaking. The ranks of American poor have swollen to the highest number (46.6 million) since poverty figures first began to be recorded, 52 years ago. The percentage of Americans who are poor (14.1 percent, or nearly one in seven) is the highest in seventeen years. Is giving so much of taxpayers' money to the state helping the poor?

. . . Those who insist that the only (or the best) way to achieve the common good is to give more resources (and more control) to the federal state, had better go looking for some evidence somewhere that undergirds their self-righteousness. They insist that others of us, who do not support the expenditure of more state money, are *immoral*.

Yet the *first* moral obligation, Blaise Pascal wrote, is to think clearly. And with evidence.

What is true for the common good is also true for social justice. Those who insist that the test of social justice is giving more tax revenues to the state need to display their evidence.

For myself, a mountain of evidence convinces me that Thomas Sowell is right: Giving money to the state in order to help the poor is a little like trying to feed the swallows by feeding the horses. The swallows get very little out of it.[4]

Similarly, in an interview with the German magazine *Spiegel International*, Kenyan economist James Shikwati pleaded with the West to stop the aid—"for God's sake."

SPIEGEL: Mr. Shikwati, the G8 summit at Gleneagles is about to beef up the development aid for Africa . . .

Shikwati: . . . for God's sake, please just stop.

SPIEGEL: Stop? The industrialized nations of the West want to eliminate hunger and poverty.

Shikwati: Such intentions have been damaging our continent for the past 40 years. If the industrial nations really want to help the Africans, they should finally terminate this awful aid. The countries that have collected the most development aid are also the ones that are in the worst shape. Despite the billions that have poured in to Africa, the continent remains poor.

SPIEGEL: Do you have an explanation for this paradox?

Shikwati: Huge bureaucracies are financed (with the aid money), corruption and complacency are promoted, Africans are taught to be beggars and not to be independent. In addition, development aid weakens the local markets everywhere and dampens the spirit of entrepreneurship that we so desperately need. As absurd as it may sound: Development aid is one of the reasons for Africa's problems. If the West were to cancel these payments, normal Africans wouldn't even notice. Only the functionaries would be hard hit. Which is why they maintain that the world would stop turning without this development aid.[5]

It is a great irony that many who champion social justice hold to statist, redistributionist approaches to poverty fighting, when the evidence is overwhelming that these approaches harm the poor by fostering a spirit of entitlement and dependency. These advocates reject approaches that have proven wildly successful in lifting millions out of poverty, simply because such approaches don't align with their core ideological commitments.

What are these approaches that have proven so successful? Consider the following from Steve Chapman's article "Toward the Conquest of World Poverty":

In 1981, 70 percent of those in the developing world subsisted on the equivalent of less than $2 a day, and 42 percent had to manage with less than $1 a day. Today, 43 percent are below $2 a day and 14 percent below $1.

"Poverty reduction of this magnitude is unparalleled in history: Never before have so many people been lifted out of poverty over such a brief period of time," write Brookings Institution researchers Laurence Chandy and Geoffrey Gertz.

Just as important as the extent of the improvement is the location: everywhere. In the past there has been improvement in a few countries or a continent. Not this time.

China has continued the rapid upward climb it began three decades ago. India, long a laggard, has shaken off its torpor. Latin America has made sharp inroads against poverty. "For the first time since 1981," says the World Bank, "we have seen less than half the population of sub-Saharan Africa living below $1.25 a day."

The start of most global trends is hard to pinpoint. This one, however, had its big bang in the early 1970s, in Chile. After a socialist government brought on economic chaos, the military seized power in a bloody coup and soon embarked on a program of drastic reform—privatizing state enterprises, fighting inflation, opening up foreign trade and investment and unshackling markets.

It was the formula offered by economists associated with the University of Chicago, notably Milton Friedman, and it turned Chile into a rare Latin American success. In time, it also facilitated a return to democracy. Chile was proof that freeing markets and curbing state control could generate broad-based prosperity, which socialist policies could only promise.

If that experiment weren't sufficient, it got another try on a much bigger scale when China's Deng Xiaoping abandoned the disastrous policies of Mao Zedong and veered onto the capitalist road. The result was an economic miracle yielding growth rates that averaged 10 percent per year.

The formula was too effective to be ignored. Over the past two decades, poorer nations have dismantled command-and control methods and given markets greater latitude. Economic growth, not redistribution, has been the surest cure for poverty, and economic freedom has been the key that unlocked the riddle of economic growth. . . .

Among many people a generation ago—and among a few today—free markets and private property were seen as the cause of poverty. But the number of adherents has dwindled in the face of repeated refutation.

As Chapman concludes, "Even communists eventually have to make peace with reality."[6]

A relatively new organization, PovertyCure, may well be the organization that changes the terms of the debate. Their short, hard-hitting video "From Aid to Enterprise" demonstrates what is at stake in the discussion.[7]

PovertyCure's mission statement begins:

PovertyCure is an international network of organizations and individuals seeking to ground our common battle against global poverty in a proper understanding of the human person and society, and to encourage solutions that foster opportunity and unleash the entrepreneurial spirit that already fills the developing world.[8]

As PovertyCure acknowledges, good intentions do not end poverty. In fact, poverty-relieving programs designed by the heart rather than the head often have unintended consequences: dependency and more poverty.

SOCIAL JUSTICE AND CULTURE

The final thing to understand about social justice is this: the root of injustice is cultural, not economic. Most people wrongly think that injustice is rooted in a lack of resources. As we have seen, when people function from the mindset of a closed system, resources are seen as limited, economics becomes a zero-sum proposition, and the only way to achieve social justice is to redistribute scarce resources.

But lack of resources is not the main cause of social injustice. The main cause lies in the dimension of culture.

Consider Haiti, for example. The day before the 2010 earthquake, ten thousand mission agencies and relief-and-development organizations and tens of thousands of volunteers were working in Haiti. Financial aid was pouring into the country—one billion dollars per year from the international community and three billion from the Haitian diaspora in the United States, Canada, and Europe.

Since the earthquake, an *additional* 1.8 billion dollars in private aid has been sent to Haiti (not including plans by the international community to raise five billion more). Haiti was a calamity before the earthquake. Two years after the earthquake, Haiti is still a calamity, notwithstanding all the good efforts of individuals, private voluntary organizations, and the international community. If Haiti's problem were a lack of resources, Haiti would be a functioning middle-class nation today.

Not only has the nation been inundated with billions of dollars in aid and the help of thousands of organizations; it has also been evangelized. Churches abound. Bible schools and seminaries are training pastors and theologians. If evangelism and church planting were the keys to Haiti's problems, Haiti would be prospering.

So why is Haiti still poor? The problem with Haiti is the voodoo mindset of its people. Haiti has been described as 80 percent Catholic, 20 percent Protestant, and 100 percent voodoo. As an animistic worldview, voodoo does not provide a framework for a family, community, or nation to develop. Animists believe that supernatural forces beyond our control determine humanity's fate. Therefore, the majority of Haitians see themselves as powerless to change the circumstances in which they find themselves—so they do not try. Instead, they wait for outside forces to bring development. In this case, the mentality of fatalism leads to the impoverishment of the nation. Bible schools may teach biblical stories or even the flow of biblical history. Seminaries may teach theology and denominational distinctions. But unless the strongholds of the mind are broken (see 2 Cor. 10:4–5), Haiti's people—Christian and non-Christian alike—will be bound by the mental stronghold of voodoo. The culture is being shaped by voodoo rather than by Christ and the biblical worldview that comports with reality.

Most aid organizations seek to mitigate the suffering caused by institutional, moral, and natural evil rather than attacking the cultural framework that creates the poverty in the first place. Mission organizations seek to deal simply with the "spiritual condition" of the Haitian people without realizing that the soul is firmly attached to the body and that the gospel needs to have a wholistic reach. It must transform all of each person—heart, soul, mind, and strength—and all of their relationships.

Culture is a product of cult (worship). If a people change their worship, say from voodoo to Christianity, a change in culture must follow. The original cultural mandate is recorded in Genesis.

> Then God said, "Let us make mankind in our image, in our likeness, so that they may rule over the fish in the sea and the birds in the sky, over the livestock and all the wild animals, and over all the creatures that move along the ground." So God created mankind in his own image, in the image of God he created them; male and female he created them. God blessed them and said to them, "Be fruitful and increase in number; fill the earth and subdue it. Rule over the fish in the sea and the birds in the sky and over every living creature that moves on the ground." (Gen. 1:26–28)

Christians and Jews understand that people have been placed on earth to create culture, to take what God has provided and make it flourish. Haiti is waiting for its people to embrace this understanding of life and discard the cultural mindsets of fatalism and poverty.

The spiritual realm impacts the physical realm through culture. When people come to Christ, their culture is to be reformed. Following that, the laws, structures, and institutions of society need to be rebuilt. Faith rooted in truth must produce godly culture, and godly culture must redeem the social, economic, and political institutions of society. This is true social justice.

Admittedly, cultures change gradually. A century or more may pass while a new idea takes root and bears fruit. Yet history indicates that cultures have changed in much less time. England experienced powerful transformation in the mid-eighteenth and early nineteenth centuries under the influence of the Wesleys (John and Charles) and the Clapham Sect, of which William Wilberforce was a leader. The Protestant Reformation altered national life in northern Europe in a few decades and proceeded to impact the world for centuries. Thomas Cahill, in his excellent book *How the Irish Saved Civilization*, relates the profound and lasting difference wrought in Ireland by the humble courage of Saint Patrick, the "apostle of Ireland."

The God who breathes new life into human societies does so through common grace as well as through the proclamation and demonstration of the gospel. Everywhere that God's image-bearing creatures establish dominion, the potential for true development exists. That is not to affirm a perfectionist humanism rooted in secular materialism. God, not humanity, is both the measure and the means of moral achievement and cultural improvement. On the other hand, none of this argument is aimed to promote the triumphalism of some Christians.

The parable of the wheat and the tares (Matt. 13:24–30) indicates that the kingdom of darkness and the kingdom of light are growing concurrently. No one can deny the evil growing at both the personal and institutional levels. Indeed, evil *is* personal. The devil is real. The "rulers and authorities in the heavenly realms" (Eph. 3:10) invade the social, economic, and political structures of societies through culture. Thus, our battle is on both the spiritual and the cultural levels. The root of society is in the cult, or worship, of the people. This is why Christians must reflect the threefold culture of God's nature: truth, beauty, and goodness. This is also why Christians must engage the workplace and the public square to influence the policies and programs of a society's institutions. Again, we do so humbly. Our weapons—service, self-sacrificing love, and prayer— are bringing down mental strongholds. Jesus sends us as servants, not masters.

For example, consider the arena of technology. This is just one domain in which Christ followers should be making a difference. On the one hand, technology is the natural extension of the cultural mandate to "tend the garden." In this way it is a blessing. In fact, many of the technological advances of history were driven by the Judeo-Christian worldview. The biblical worldview called human beings to apply the lessons of science, through technology, to the ravages caused by the fall. The biblical value of the dignity of humans motivated people to find ways to ease distressing human toil, to lift precious humans from drudgery. Vishal Mangalwadi notes, "It was the Bible that made the medieval West the first civilization in history that did not rest on the backs of sweating slaves."[9] But cut loose from a biblical foundation, technology can become a curse. Our problem today is the severing of science and technology from the metaphysical and moral framework of the Bible. Too often the only question asked is "Can we do it?" while "Should we do it?" is seldom considered. We need to ask the moral questions in the development and use of technology, both at a personal and corporate level.

While we do not expect a perfected society on this side of the completed kingdom of God, a biblical engagement at the level of culture should bring what Francis Schaeffer called "substantial healing" in every area of life.

THE GREAT COMMISSION AND CULTURAL TRANSFORMATION

Many Christians see church growth as the primary, if not the exclusive, solution to cultural influence. Some point to the rapid growth of the church in the global South as the paradigm for changing the world. While the growth of the church in the South is something to celebrate, we suffer from a truncated view of the Great Commission. To consider church growth to be the ultimate solution to cultural redemption is to ignore the overwhelming data. In our day we have more churches than ever before, but if church planting alone were the means of cultural transformation, we should have seen a global impact on societies by now. The church growth movement has been successful in what it set out to do. Sadly, it did not set out to do the right thing. We have preached the gospel of salvation (saving souls and rapidly planting churches) but not the gospel Jesus preached, the gospel of the kingdom (Mark 1:15; Luke 4:43; 8:1; see also Matt. 28:18–20).

Notwithstanding these realities, for three reasons we remain optimistic about the future. First, Christ won the defining battle of the entire spiritual war, the battle of the cross (Col. 1:15–20). So we know with certainty how the cosmic conflict will end. Second, Christ will return at the end of history for his bride (Rev. 19:6–7) to complete the task that he started (Rev. 21:3–4). This is the ultimate framework for our lives and the reason that we as Christians should be the most optimistic people. Finally, God works in history, promising to bless all nations through Abraham. As he has worked in the past, he can work today to bring cultural change.

A culture will be transformed only through revival[10] and reformation.[11] Revival without reformation is not true revival—it doesn't last. A culture will not be transformed by evangelists and teachers alone. Profound and broad change will require "ordinary" Christians to think theologically and live within the framework of truth, that is, the Judeo-Christian worldview. This includes businesspeople creating a thriving economic order; doctors and nurses increasing the health of communities; artists and architects bringing beauty into the home, marketplace, and public square; scientists and technicians pushing back the ravages of natural evil (e.g., preparing Haiti to withstand the next earthquake); farmers and agriculturalists producing more and healthier food within the context of land stewardship; and the list goes on.

One fine example of an ordinary Christian who brought transformation to his society is Arthur Guinness (1725–1803), founder of Guinness Brewery, whose story Stephen Mansfield tells in *The Search for God and Guinness*.[12] For Guinness, Christ's call had two sides, the call of the cross to salvation and the call to work as part of a godly commitment to engage culture. Arthur Guinness and his employees labored hard and worked with excellence. They worked to the glory of God. This attitude toward the sacredness of work propelled the Guinness brand to become what is widely regarded today as the world's best and most famous beer. The Guinness wealth was then used to benefit others, both inside and outside the company.

Employees were blessed in many ways: wages 10–20 percent higher than the Irish average, medical and dental care, retirement plans funded entirely by the company without employee contributions, savings opportunities, and educational offerings, to name just a few.

Guinness was also generous to the community. The company

- sponsored guilds, from associations for the care of animals and the establishment of gardens, to athletic unions to encourage health and fitness;
- championed the rights of Roman Catholics (even though Guinness himself was a nonconformist Protestant);
- brought medical care to poor people via Guinness's position on the board of Meath Hospital;
- fought for the abolition of dueling;
- supported charities that promoted Gaelic art and culture;
- founded the first Sunday schools in all of Ireland;
- founded the Guinness Trust to provide housing for the "laboring poor";
- hired Dr. John Lumsden to do public health surveys in communities where Guinness factories were located, and developed policies and programs to increase public health.

As with Arthur Guinness and the Guinness Corporation, we should apply the biblical paradigm and principles—both personally and corporately—to policies and programs that seek social justice. In concert with this, Oswald Chambers writes, "Never look for justice in this world, but never cease to give it."[13] In a fallen world, we will always face injustice. But as Christians, we should spend more time extending justice to others and less time demanding justice for ourselves.

CHAPTER 3

THE DEMISE OF
SOCIAL JUSTICE

A s a voice for social justice in another era, Robert Ellis Thompson (1844–1924), professor of mathematics, social science, and theology at the University of Pennsylvania, stated: "You can judge the scale on which any scheme of help for the needy stands by this single quality: Does it make great demands on men to give themselves to their brethren?"[1]

Take a moment to reflect on this. According to Thompson, the critical measure of compassion in a previous generation was the demand it made on those who would help others. How times have changed! We need to examine how our definition of social justice has degenerated from compassion rooted in a biblical worldview into pity rooted in the modern atheistic-materialistic framework.

COMPASSION BEFORE

Economist and political philosopher Thomas Sowell writes, "'Compassion' has become one of a growing number of politicized words (like 'access' or 'diversity') whose meaning has been corrupted beyond redemption."[2]

Sowell is correct that the word *compassion* has been corrupted—it is merely a shadow of its past glory—but it is not beyond redemption. Compassion is the very nature of God. Although the glory of the word's meaning has been greatly diminished in the modern world, the word and its powerful action will never disappear because God, who is compassion, is not going anywhere.

It is a sociological maxim that you must change language before changing culture. And a shift in worldview is the precursor to a shift in language and culture. The pattern can be drawn like this:

WORLDVIEW SHIFT → LANGUAGE SHIFT →
CULTURE SHIFT → POLICY SHIFT →
PROGRAMMATIC SHIFT

Centuries ago, compassion was used as a verb: to compassionate. It was the act of journeying with other individuals in their pain and passion. It was to enter their world, to "walk in their moccasins," to join with them in times of difficulty, to share with them in their misery—to commiserate. Anthony Ashley Cooper, the third earl of Shaftesbury, wrote in the eighteenth century: "To compassionate, i.e., to join with in passion. . . . To commiserate, i.e., to join with in misery. . . . This in one order of life is right and good; nothing more harmonious; and to be without this, or not to feel this, is unnatural, horrid, immane [monstrous]."[3]

This view of compassion as a verb was rooted in the biblical narrative, in the nature of God himself. God is called "the compassionate" (Exod. 34:5–6). He walked with Adam and Eve in the garden of Eden (Gen. 3:8). He commissioned the building of a tabernacle so that he could "dwell among" his people (Exod. 25:8; 29:44–46). Above all, God chose to incarnate himself, to live in the midst of his people on earth (John 1:14). The God of the universe humbled himself and took on the form of a man (Phil. 2:7–9). The writer to the Hebrews affirms that, yes, Jesus Christ is a faithful high priest, that is, one who has been tempted as we have (Heb. 4:15). He knows the human predicament intimately. The transcendent Creator of the universe, the fountainhead of compassion, is also the intimate God who acts to compassionate and commiserate with his people.

Christ's followers are to see compassion as a verb, not a noun. Compassion in not merely a feeling; it is an attitude involving action. Jesus gave us a wonderful illustration of this truth.

In the lead-up to the parable of the good Samaritan (Luke 10:25–29), we see something both remarkable and subtle. An expert in the Jewish law asks Jesus, "What must I do to inherit eternal life?" Jesus responds by asking the scholar, "What is written in the Law?" The lawyer responds correctly that we are to love God and love our neighbor. Acknowledging the lawyer's correct answer, Jesus says in effect, "Now go do it!" The lawyer knows he is not doing what the law requires, so to justify himself, he asks Jesus, "And who is my neighbor?" (Note that the lawyer uses *neighbor* as a noun.)

Jesus then tells the story of the good Samaritan (Luke 10:30–35). A priest and a Levite each pass the broken man beside the road and ask in effect, "Is this my neighbor?" They have never seen him before, so they conclude they have no obligation to help. Then the Samaritan comes. He asks a different question: "Is this someone who needs neighboring?" The answer is yes, and Jesus goes on to describe the Samaritan's nine acts of compassion toward the Jew.

Following this description of God's compassion, Jesus asks, "Which of these three do you think was a neighbor to the man who fell into the hands of robbers?" (Luke 10:36). Jesus applies the word *neighbor* to the Samaritan rather than to the broken man. In doing so, he changes the sense of the word from a noun ("who is my neighbor?") to a verb ("who acted in a neighborly fashion?"). The lawyer answers, "The one who had mercy on him" (Luke 10:37). Thus, the lawyer understands that compassion is action. Jesus says to him, "Go and do likewise."

Gary Haugen, founder and president of International Justice Mission (IJM), also makes this connection between compassion and action. Love is transcendent, yet it shows up in everyday behaviors.

Christians of mature faith know that love is both a deeply mystical and a profoundly practical calling. In some mysterious way, when we feed the hungry, visit the sick and clothe the naked, we do it for him also (Matthew 25). Jesus' model for love, a name-less Samaritan, messed up his clothes and his schedule by pick-ing up a stranger who lay wounded and beaten in a ditch (Luke 10). Acts of love like this are so important to God that when the Israelites couldn't be bothered with the workaday practicali-ties of what it takes "to loose the chains of injustice" and "to set the oppressed free," God stopped listening to their prayers (Isa. 58:1–6).[4]

God's nature is compassion. He acts compassionately and expects his people to do the same. True social justice is joining people who are in need and poverty and acting to help them. To commiserate is to be in such a relationship with a person so as to share in his or her misery.

This understanding was the definition of compassion for previous generations. At one time, most people in the West still acknowledged God's existence and defined every aspect of their lives in relation to God. Noah Webster's 1828 *American Dictionary of the English Language*, the defining dictionary of America's founding,[5] defines compassion as "a suf-fering with another; painful sympathy." The *Oxford English Dictionary*, first published in 1884, defines compassion as "suffering together with another, participating in suffering." Intrinsic to both definitions is being in relationship with someone in her suffering and poverty. It is knowing her and acting compassionately toward her. Sympathy is a feeling; com-passion is a moral attitude, a belief that drives one to action. Sympathy centers around feeling good; compassion centers around doing good.

Christians of an earlier age demonstrated this. The members of the Clapham Sect in England showed compassion toward women and chil-dren working in sweatshops, inmates in English prisons, and black slaves being shipped by the tens of thousands to the shores of the Americas and the plantations of the Caribbean. This group of men and women acted to bring about labor and prison reform and to end slavery. Zachary Macaulay (1768–1838) was a member of the Clapham Sect and a leader of the abo-litionist movement. In order to experience what the slaves experienced in their journey across the Atlantic, he booked passage on a slave ship. He personally shared in the slaves' misery so that he could better represent his fellow human beings in the fight for their emancipation.

As a tribute to this commiserator with slaves, a bust of Macaulay was placed in Westminster Abbey, along with a medallion that conveyed the motto of the abolitionist movement. The medallion pictures a kneeling slave asking, "Am I not a man and a brother?" The words engraved on the memorial reflect Macaulay's understanding of the true nature of social justice:

In grateful remembrance of Zachary Macaulay, who, during a protracted life, with an intense but quiet perseverance which no success could relax, no reverse could subdue, no toil, privation, or reproach could daunt, devoted his time, talents, fortune, and all the energies of his mind and body to the service of the most injured and helpless of mankind: and who partook for more than forty successive years, in the counsels and in the labours which guided and blest by God first rescued the British Empire from the guilt of the slave trade; and finally conferred freedom on eight hundred thousand slaves; This tablet is erected by those who drew wisdom from his mind, and a lesson from his life, and who now humbly rejoice in the assurance, that through the Divine Redeemer, the foundation of all his hopes, he shares in the happiness of those who rest from their labours, and whose works do follow them. He was born at Inverary, N.B. [North Britain] on the 2 May 1768: and died in London on the 13 May 1838.

Another example of compassion comes from the German count Nikolaus Ludwig von Zinzendorf (1700–1760). When Zinzendorf was nineteen, he toured Europe, a common rite of passage for young aristocrats of his time. In Dusseldorf, the young count viewed Domenico Feti's painting *Ecce Homo* ("Behold the Man"), which depicts the crucified Christ. At the bottom of the painting, Feti attributes these words to Jesus: "This have I done for you—What will you do for me?"

These words were a knife in young Zinzendorf's heart, as if Christ were speaking directly to him. From that day he dedicated his life to the service of Christ. In May 1727 he opened his estate at Herrnhut to shelter the poor and the displaced, an example of social justice in its fullest sense. Many who came as refugees were Christians, and more became Christians. From this group grew an unbroken prayer movement—24 hours a day, 365 days a year—that lasted over one hundred years. This prayer operation birthed one of the greatest missionary movements in the modern world: the Moravians.

The compassionate and commiserative lives of the Moravians inspired William Carey, the father of modern missions, to go to India. It was also the Moravians' example that gave John and Charles Wesley their wholistic vision for preaching the gospel, which brought about the social transformation of England during the 1700s.

"COMPASSION" TODAY

That was then. In the ensuing years, our world and our words have changed. We have moved from the worship of the compassionate God, who made people in his own image and who joins with us in our misery, to an atheistic framework in which human beings are animals and only the fittest deserve to survive. In this framework the meaning of the word *compassion* has changed. Webster's 2010 *New World College Dictionary* reflects this change, defining compassion as "sorrow for the sufferings or trouble of another or others, accompanied by an urge to help; deep sympathy; pity."

Consider some other current treatments of the word *compassion*:

- "A feeling of wanting to help someone who is sick, hungry, in trouble, etc."[6]
- "A strong feeling of sympathy and sadness for other people's suffering or bad luck and a desire to help."[7]
- "Sympathetic pity and concern for the sufferings or misfortunes of others."[8]
- "Compassion makes us feel good."[9]

In everyday discourse, too, we can note the shift in language:

FROM	TO
Humans are made in the image of God	Humans are highly evolved animals
Suffering with	Pity or sentimentality
Doing good	Feeling good
Sharing self, time, and talents	Giving money (to relieve guilt)

Why has our understanding of compassion shifted? Because our worldview has shifted. Our fundamental view of life and the world (i.e., our worship) defines our culture. Culture and language are intimately tied together, and language establishes our understanding of compassion. Ideas have consequences! If there is no God in the universe, if all of life is merely the product of material, cause-and-effect processes, the concept of compassion is radically changed, indeed deformed, and without foundation. Where is the distinction between cruelty and compassion? When the mantra is "the survival of the fittest," where does compassion fit? It is mere sentiment! If there is no underlying morality and meaning in life, all we can do is pity those who have it worse off than we do—because that pity makes *us* feel better.

THE ROOT OF POVERTY

STUDY GUIDE
SESSION 7

As a society pursues a shift in worldview, its language and culture will change as well. These changes lead to a shift in the policies and practices of compassion. (Recall the diagram on page 32.)

Over the past two hundred years, the worldview in the West has shifted from Judeo-Christian theism to deism to secular humanism (and is shifting again to neo-paganism, a subject for another book).[10] Compassion, once defined by a biblical worldview, has been reframed by a secular-humanist worldview.

Three Booths

Three nineteenth-century figures, all sharing the name Booth, demonstrate the pivotal shift in principles, policies, and programs related to caring for the poor.

William Booth (1829–1912) was a Methodist minister. He and his wife Catherine Booth (1829–90) founded the East London Christian Mission in 1865. The ministry began by not only preaching to the poor but also calling them to repentance and transformation. The Booths understood that the root of poverty was the sin *inside* human beings. By preaching Christ crucified and calling people to repent from sin, William and Catherine were laying the foundation for people to escape poverty. In 1878 their organization changed its name to the Salvation Army. This Protestant Christian church, with its emphasis on walking with the poor (*com-passion*, "to suffer with"), has grown into a global movement working in 120 countries.

Charles Booth (1840–1916, no relation to William) was an English philanthropist, researcher, and social reformer. He was a Unitarian, which put him squarely on the deistic bridge between biblical theism and secularism. He combined the classic virtues of hard work, dependability, and thrift with modern scientific social research into the causes of poverty. His research on the poor working class in London led to government intervention in the fight against poverty. This move from personal responsibility to government responsibility created a titanic shift in Western society's understanding of and solutions to poverty. It is here that the term *social justice* was decoupled from a biblical frame and from its synonym *compassion*.

These two streams of Booths—William and Catherine on the one hand, and Charles on the other—represent the divergence in modern understandings of helping the poor. Catherine and William worked from a biblical worldview, which recognizes the root of poverty as sin. They understood the influence of a poverty mentality and the consequences of foolish behavior, including alienation from family and increased poverty. To solve the problem of poverty, one had to go to the root and call people to repentance, to a new mind and new life in Christ.

While Charles Booth also recognized the need for virtuous rather than foolish behavior, the deistic framework of his research and policy recommendations began to shift the locus of responsibility from the individual to external institutions. This ultimately led to today's practice, in which the government is seen as the primary authority responsible for addressing the needs of the poor. In deistic thinking, the Creator is transcendent, but is not engaged in the world. To a deist, God is not the incarnate Christ who engages personally in people's lives; he is non-incarnate and distant. So the model of personal engagement is lost in impersonal and institutional solutions to issues of poverty.

Greeley vs. Raymond

This transition in the meaning of compassion continued across the Atlantic Ocean in a series of debates between two American newspapermen in the 1840s. Horace Greeley (1811–72), the founder and editor of the *New York Tribune,* subscribed to a deistic worldview with universalist application. Henry Raymond (1820–69), the founder of the *New York Times* and a Presbyterian, held a Judeo-Christian worldview. The debate between these two revolved around their views of humanity, the nature of poverty, and how best to provide charity.

In his book *The Tragedy of American Compassion,* Marvin Olasky describes how these divergent belief systems led to very different understandings of compassion. Greeley believed that poverty was *external* to man. The inherent needs of humans, he said, are

good in themselves. Evil flows only from their repression or subversion. Give them full scope, free play, a perfect and complete development, and universal happiness must be the result. . . . Create a new form of Society in which this shall be possible . . . then you will have a perfect Society; then you will have "the Kingdom of Heaven." . . . The heart of man is not depraved . . . his passions do not prompt to wrong doing, and do not therefore by their action, produce evil.[11]

Greeley argued from a romanticized, naturalistic worldview. He argued that humans are naturally good; it is the institutions and structures of society that are evil and thus bring poverty. Build a new form of society, and poverty would be eradicated. We would have heaven on earth.

Raymond, by contrast, argued that the cause of poverty was, at its core, *internal*, rooted in "the sinfulness of the heart of man." Olasky writes, "The remedy, [Raymond] argued, must reach that cause, or it must prove inefficient. The heart must change. The law of Man's nature must cease to be the supreme law of his life. He must learn to subject that law to the higher law of righteousness, revealed in his conscience and in the Word of God. . . . And that subjugation can only be effected by his personal will, the supernatural aids furnished in the Christian Scheme."[12]

Raymond saw the root of poverty as being *inside* the human heart. Any solution to poverty must begin with a "heart transplant," or a new birth, as Jesus said. It begins with repentance, with owning one's sin and—in the power of Christ's life within—living within the moral framework of the universe. Unless you deal with the human heart, you will not get to the root of poverty.

The debate between Greeley and Raymond illustrates the two very different ways of seeing poverty and its human causes and consequences. Raymond's view aligns with what the ancients understood: we live in a moral universe, and sin dwells inside each human being. Moderns like Charles Booth and Horace Greeley naively held that the human heart is pure and society perfectible.

As paradigms have shifted over time, so has language. Michael Harrington, author of *The Other America: Poverty in the United States* (published in 1962), was the first to write about *structural poverty*. His premise was that people are poor because they have been deprived by the controlling structures of society. To be sure, structural poverty does exist. So does, for example, institutional evil. But institutional evil is just one of the three forms of evil, the other two being personal (or moral) and natural. To focus on institutional evil while ignoring personal and natural evil would be ineffective at best, and perhaps counterproductive. In any case, the recognition of structural poverty in a society should not negate the root of all poverty: personal sin, for which individual responsibility must be taken.

Dependency Theory

Another language shift came from sociologist Fernando Cardosa, who advanced the concept of dependency theory in the 1970s. This social theory is built on a closed-system or zero-sum model of economics. According to dependency theorists, resources are finite and fixed. These scarce resources flow from a "periphery" of poor and underdeveloped "Southern" nations to a "core" of wealthy, Western nations. The latter are enriched at the expense of the former. A shift in language, such as the coining of the new phrase "dependency theory," reflects a shift in worldview and ends up redefining the nature of poverty in the modern mind and encouraging the expansion of socialist schemes.

Socialism seeks to take from the rich and spread the wealth around evenly. There is no room in this framework for people who are impoverished to create and use their own wealth. The solution to poverty is the redistribution of wealth from the rich to the poor. This concept has been embraced by modern thinkers, including many Christians. Some well-meaning Christ followers make the untenable conclusion, based on socialism's zero-sum economic model, that reduced discretionary spending by wealthy citizens would transfer money to poorer citizens.

For example, Ken Wytsma writes, "In 2001, Americans spent more than $450 billion on holiday shopping—more than the annual GDP of either Sweden or Saudi Arabia. The World Bank estimates that to provide everyone in the world with clean water for drinking and sanitation would cost up to $21 billion each year. This ever-expanding chasm between the developed and developing world is not the good news of Christmas or the gospel."[13] Although I agree with much of Ken Wytsma's general philosophy on social justice, this particular passage exemplifies the zero-sum mindset. The implication is that people in developing countries don't have water because Americans are self-absorbed and spend so much on holiday shopping. Yes, materialism and narcissism in America, and increasingly elsewhere, are destructive. But the notion of an "ever-expanding chasm" is not borne out by the facts. Such a concept has become a truism for people on the political left who are heavily influenced by Marxist or socialist economic thinking—including Christians.

While the crass consumerism found in the West is not to be defended, we must be careful not to target consumerism per se as the root of poverty in the developing world. In many countries where free-market principles and disciplines are taking hold, the middle class is growing. (Once again, it is important to recognize that neither the opulent, throwaway culture of the West nor the poverty in the global South is the result of behavior derived from a truly biblical worldview.)

In practice, dependency theory disempowers the poor and actually increases dependency. Why? Because instead of fostering internal self-government and entrepreneurship among individuals, redistribution rewards slothfulness and penalizes personal responsibility. As the West moved from its roots in a Judeo-Christian paradigm to the modern atheistic paradigm, the result was a radical deforming of principle, policy, and program. The ancient principle, that poverty is rooted in the sinful heart and sinful behavior, was abandoned for the new principle, that poverty is rooted solely outside the human heart in the laws and institutions of society. New policies and programs followed. The rise of Darwinism to justify an atheistic faith led not only to biological applications but also to social applications in the form of social Darwinism. Darwin's theory of evolution applies not only in biology; it is a comprehensive ideology that infects all of life, including social, economic, and political theory—and practice, too.

New paradigms and principles stimulated the rise of the welfare state in the form of socioeconomic/sociopolitical systems (e.g., Marxism and socialism) as attempts to deal with poverty. As a secular-humanist worldview displaced the Judeo-Christian worldview, two new emphases for dealing with poverty arose within Christendom. One was liberation theology, based on Marxist political and economic theory, which seeks to liberate people trapped in poverty by economic and/or political oppression. The other was the social gospel, which seeks to eliminate poverty by reforming society according to "Christian" principles, often without acknowledging that the human heart must be transformed.

When people are not responsible for their behavior, they diminish in stature. They become small. As the government takes responsibility for poverty, it grows large at the expense of human significance and freedom. People become wards of the state. Individuals lose their responsibility for their own education, material well-being, or health. Instead, the government becomes responsible for these things.

In addition, if men and women do not govern themselves internally by moral principles, they will be governed externally by ever-increasing laws, courts, and prisons. In such a scenario, the individual is imprisoned, and the state becomes the prison warden. The words of Leo Tolstoy are instructive:

> Not only does the action of Governments not deter men from crimes; on the contrary, it increases crime by always disturbing and lowering the moral standard of society. Nor can this be otherwise, since always and everywhere a Government, by its very nature, must put in the place of the highest, eternal, religious law (not written in books but in the hearts of men, and binding on every one) its own unjust, man-made laws, the object of which is neither justice nor the common good of all but various considerations of home and foreign expediency.[14]

We must remind ourselves that humans, not institutions, are created in God's image. And humans, not institutions, will live forever. As C. S. Lewis said, "There are no ordinary people. You have never talked to a mere mortal. Nations, cultures, arts, civilizations—these are mortal, and their life is to ours as the life of a gnat."[15]

CHAPTER 4

HOW A CORRUPTED WORSHIP ADULTERATED OUR COMPASSION

A s we have seen, culture is a product of cult (worship). We build societies in the image of the god we worship. The psalmist put it this
way:

STUDY GUIDE SESSION 8

> The idols of the nations are silver and gold,
> > made by human hands.
> They have mouths, but cannot speak;
> > eyes, but cannot see;
> They have ears, but cannot hear,
> > nor is there breath in their mouths.
> Those who make them will be like them,
> > and so will all who trust in them. (Ps. 135:15–18)

Likewise, Marvin Olasky reminds us, "Cultures build systems of
charity in the image of the god they worship."[1] This truth is reflected in
the three distinct models of compassion today. The biblical worldview has
given rise to Judeo-Christian social teaching. The atheistic worldview has
birthed two models: social universalism and its pessimistic counterpart,
social Darwinism.

MODELS OF COMPASSION

Judeo-Christian Social Teaching

Judeo-Christian social teaching is the application of a comprehensive moral philosophy found in the Old and New Testaments. God cares about each human being and all aspects of life. God's agenda is wholistic healing. Christians should thus be concerned about the causes of and solutions to all forms of poverty. Olasky describes four principles of the biblical social framework,[2] which I have paraphrased as follows.

First, God is Creator. He has established a creation order, a framework for healthy living. He personally intervened in history to bring healing to those who violate his order. It follows that human beings are to personally intervene to help the poor.

Second, because God loves human beings, he chose to walk in our world, to be in relationship with us. "The Word became flesh and made his dwelling among us" (John 1:14). This precludes charity done at arm's length. It is better and more God-like to know people in their poverty, to become familiar with them and their families as individuals. Pastor Ken Wytsma points out that this value placed on relationships is grounded in Scripture:

> In English, we translate the Hebrew words *tsedek* and *mishpat* as either "righteousness" or as "justice" depending on the context. This is because the Hebrew sense of the words *tsedek* and *mishpat* linked the personal and communal components of "just" or "righteous" living. . . .
>
> Dr. Gerry Breshears, a theology professor at Western Seminary in Portland, explains that the Hebrew word *tsedek* means: a life in which all relationships—human to human, human to God, and human to creation—are well-ordered and harmonious. . . . *Tsedek* is both a personal virtue and a communal imperative.[3]

Third, God's laws govern the universe. Poverty comes from violating God's order. If people are to be lifted out of poverty, they must be taught to obey all that Jesus commanded (Matt. 28:20).

Fourth, sometimes the most compassionate act is withholding help. We create dependency when we give charity to those who are able but not willing to help themselves. We leave them enslaved to their vices.

In the Judeo-Christian scheme, the *giver* was not merely a *donor* of money but someone who shared his or her time, talent, and treasure. Both parties benefited from the arrangement: the poor person received an opportunity to lift himself or herself out of poverty, and the benefactor grew through "suffering together" with another human being. The charity was connected to the virtue of the Protestant ethic of laboring, saving, and giving, which established life patterns that lifted people out of poverty.

Social Universalism

Social universalism is a specious type of optimistic humanism, a sentimentality toward the poor. Many social universalists are altruistic; they live for others. But they proclaim love of mankind without a love for God. Beatrice (Potter) Webb (1858–1943) is an example of a social universalist. She wrote of her optimistic humanist convictions in her diary: "Towards humanity, who is the only true Great Being, we, the conscious elements of whom she is the compound, shall henceforth direct every aspect of our life, individual and collective. Our thoughts will be devoted to the knowledge of humanity, our affections to the Love, our actions to her service."[4]

In the universalist's world, consciousness of sin shifts from personal sin and individual responsibility to class consciousness and group responsibility. The wealthy class created poverty, universalists say, so it is their responsibility to end poverty. The poor are no longer individuals and families, but rather a class of people. Individuals are not big enough to solve this class problem. Only the government is big enough to deal with poverty. Here again we see social justice decoupled from its roots in Judeo-Christian theism and paired instead with an atheistic and humanistic framework.

Social justice and its synonym, compassion, are thus redefined. To be compassionate, according to social universalism, is to support state-sponsored poverty programs. People who give sacrificially of their time, talent, and treasure to help the poor rather than promote statist redistribution are deemed, by the political elite, to be without heart, without compassion. What a remarkable irony!

Some of Beatrice Webb's contemporaries in the late Victorian era were deists living from a moral memory of their predecessors but cut loose from the biblical foundation of that morality. Working from that moral memory and a belief in science, they were personally involved in a quest for social justice. The classic example of their work is Toynbee Hall—part charity, part study program in the slums of London, founded in 1884. Renowned American historian Gertrude Himmelfarb writes about founder Samuel Barnett, whose desire was

> that the young men living among the poor would become better acquainted with them, move more easily among them, understand and sympathize with them, and serve them in whatever way they could—but not that they would live the life of the poor or lose themselves in the service of the poor. They were not to be latter-day St. Francises. On the contrary, they were to show the poor the possibility of a more elevated, more gracious, more fulfilling life, a life that the poor could not hope to emulate but that could, by its example, enrich and enlarge them.[5]

This was not truly compassionate service but rather service that maintained and even furthered a distinction between the upper and lower classes.

Liberal theologians of the era, whose presuppositions were born out of a secular-humanist worldview, attributed a sort of biblical justification to the humanist agenda. As Olasky points out, "Liberal theologian George Herron went one step further, claiming 'that the public ownership of the sources and means of production is the sole answer to the social question, and the sole basis of spiritual liberty.' . . . Their theology, labeled with public relations brilliance the 'social gospel,' emphasized God's love but not God's holiness, and thus urged charity without challenge. The materialist bias played up physical needs but was embarrassed by evangelism and spiritual need. 'Save the world but not the individual' became a motto."[6]

As the Christian memory of this generation's predecessors faded, personal involvement in compassion diminished and was replaced with writing checks. Nonprofit organizations became surrogate caregivers. Government programs, supported by taxes, replaced volunteering and personal charity. The idea that humanity is good while structures are evil led to wildly utopian visions of the future and, ironically, invested more power in central governments, which somehow escaped the evil reputation assigned to other structures and whose responsibility is to bring heaven on earth.

Social Darwinism

Social Darwinism is the logical application of survival of the fittest to the social and economic realms. It produces a class of pessimistic humanists. They are more honest than the liberal theologians, but they are also anticompassionate. Man is merely an animal; only the economically fit should survive. Herbert Spencer, the British social Darwinist who coined the phrase "survival of the fittest," wrote: "The unfit must be eliminated as nature intended, for the principle of natural selection must not be violated by the artificial preservation of these least able to take care of themselves."[7]

The Causes of Pauperism, the 1876 report to the New York State Board of Charities, stated: "The examination has made it clear that by far the greater number of paupers have reached that condition by idleness, improvidence, drunkenness, or some form of vicious indulgence. It is equally clear that these vices and weaknesses are very frequently, if not universally, the result of tendencies which are to a greater or less degree hereditary. . . . Vigorous efforts must be instituted to break the line of pauper descent."[8] Social Darwinists dehumanized the poor. Their desire was to eliminate poverty by getting rid of the poor. This is illustrated by a T-shirt in Bangladesh, produced by a nongovernmental organization, that showed a silhouette of a pregnant woman overlaid with the prohibition symbol. This graphic summarizes the goals of social Darwinism.

Social Darwinists developed in two strains: passive and proactive. The passive strain simply wanted charities to stop intervening with the poor and let nature take its course. In 1880, social Darwinist William Graham Sumner wrote: "Nature's remedies against vice are terrible. She removes the victims without pity. A drunkard in the gutter is just where he ought to be, according to the fitness and tendency of things. Nature has set up on him the process of decline and dissolution by which she removes things which have survived their usefulness."[9]

The proactive social Darwinists wanted to "help" nature, to speed up the process of the survival of the fittest by actively eliminating the poor. The eugenics movement, popular in the first half of the twentieth century, sought to employ science to get rid of those human beings deemed unworthy of life. The death camps of Adolf Hitler's Third Reich were examples of proactive social Darwinism. In the United States, Margaret Sanger, the founder of the American Birth Control League (now Planned Parenthood), led a proactive social Darwinist lobby. She sought to help evolution along by eliminating people of color, poor people, and people who were mentally handicapped, through sterilization and abortion.[10] At the beginning of the twenty-first century, social Darwinism now continues in the horrors of abortion, infanticide ("post-birth abortion"), fetal stem-cell research, and euthanasia.

THE DEMISE OF COMPASSION

The rise of atheistic Darwinism in the West did not leave our practice of compassion unscathed.

Many readers will remember seeing something like this graphic during their public school experience. It is meant to show the evolution of the horse. But the effects of teaching evolution are far greater than memories of childhood schooldays. Darwinian evolution, after all, is as much an ideology as it is science.

Most Western Christians would agree that the worldview of the West has largely shifted from Judeo-Christian theism to atheistic materialism. The most profound shift has been in our concept of ultimate reality. Where do we begin our understanding of the universe, from an

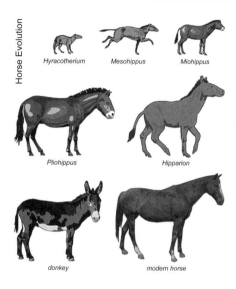

infinite and personal God or from nature? The starting point changes everything.

The shift from God to nature requires a shift in our understanding of what it means to be human. God created comprehensive beings with physical, social, intellectual, and spiritual components. But this shift has degraded humans, who are now regarded as mere physical beings. No longer are female and male seen as the image of God. Now humans are seen either as animals (the view of atheism) or machines (the vision of the Marxist state). Rather than being rational and morally responsible creatures, humans are viewed as amoral. They have no more foundation for rationality, or for compassion, than does any other animal.

The concept of men and women as sinners has largely disappeared in modern culture. Instead, we have the irrational position that in an amoral universe, human beings are by nature good. (What can "good" mean in an amoral universe?) This position dramatically changes our understanding of compassion and how we respond to poverty. The shift in ideas brought about a shift in language and, ultimately, in how we treat people who are poor.

Our view and practice of compassion have been profoundly affected by the worldview shift. The following charts depict this in five dimensions.

1. *Love of God as the Basis for Loving People*

IDEA SHIFT	LANGUAGE SHIFT
Love of God → Love of humanity alone	Moral/religious → secular
	Compassion → sentiment

The drivers for the new concept of compassion are altruism grounded in love of mankind alone, sentimentality over the plight of the poor, and emotional resentment for lack of outcomes that reflect economic equality.

2. *Personhood of the Human*

IDEA SHIFT	LANGUAGE SHIFT
Personal → Impersonal	Poor person (individual) → The poor (a class)
	Unemployed person (person) → Unemployment (a condition)

As worldviews have shifted and the concept of humanity has diminished, the understanding of poverty has changed from the plight of an individual with a name to the condition of an impersonal class.

Historian Gertrude Himmelfarb explains this shift:

> As the problem became impersonalized, so did responsibility for it. The older terms implied that the sources and causes of unemployment could be found in the individual—his character, capacity, will, situation, chance, or misfortune. The new term directed attention to the larger forces affecting the economy and the nature of the "industrial system." . . . And as responsibility for the problem became impersonalized, so did the solution. . . . A problem beyond the control of individuals could only be remedied by forces and agencies beyond the reach of individuals. For social reformers this meant the intervention of the state; for Marxists it meant a radical reconstitution of the economy.[11]

Himmelfarb points out that we are "'pauperizing' the poor by reducing the 'independent' poor to a state of dependency."[12] We see the outcome of this in the welfare system of the West. We also see it in the dependency-building enterprises of so many Western poverty programs in the developing world.[13]

3. Moral and Relational Nature of the Universe

IDEA SHIFT	LANGUAGE SHIFT
Moral → Structural	Individual responsibility → Class responsibility
	Private solutions → Public solutions

In the earlier mindset, compassion addressed a moral problem. Individuals understood that they needed to take responsibility for themselves and for their families and neighbors. They cared for the poor in their relational circles. Today, compassion addresses a structural problem. We talk about class responsibility. The shift was from a moral philosophy with private solutions (empowering people who were poor, providing them work opportunities, etc.) to a political economy requiring massive public solutions. The inevitable result was entitlement societies. Take, for example, the continuing debate in the United States on policies of "freedom before the law" and "freedom of enterprise" versus policies that build dependency and entitlement. While each side in the debate may be motivated by a desire to help those who are poor, different worldviews lead to different policies and programs to achieve that help.[14] Compassion looks very different when seen from these opposite viewpoints.

Again Himmelfarb explains:

The old remedies were "temporary expedients," whether by voluntary agencies or public authorities, which "more properly fall under the description of charity" (hence, for the earlier history of the subject, the reader was referred to the article "Charity and Charities"); the new were "permanent" remedies such as labor exchanges and unemployment insurance.[15]

"Poverty" like "unemployment," had the effect of moving the discussion from the subjective realm of persons to the objective condition that defined them. The emphasis thus shifted from the personal characteristics of the poor—their particular circumstances, characters, habits—to the impersonal causes of poverty: the state of the economy, the structure of society, the action (or inaction) of government, the institutions and forces affecting social conditions and relations.[16]

4. The Basis for Equality

IDEA SHIFT	LANGUAGE SHIFT
Equality before God/law → Equality of outcomes	Justice → (welfare) Rights
	Equity → (numerical) Equality

The shift here was away from biblical principles such as equality before God, who does not show partiality (see Deut. 10:17). These principles were articulated in the founding documents of the United States. Their public corollary was equality before the law. The framework that replaced these principles was a materialistic economy of equal outcomes. The shift was from justice to welfare rights and from treating people with equity to numerical equality.

5. Relational Participation with Poor Neighbors

IDEA SHIFT	LANGUAGE SHIFT
Sharing time and self → Sharing money	Relationships → Dollars

Another shift was from the relational to the impersonal. In the old system of charity, people personally engaged with their poor neighbors. They shared their time and talents as well as their treasure. But the new charity separates people into donors and recipients. The former can stay safe in their isolated communities. Giving dollars has replaced knowing

people. Instead of spending time with poor people, we spend time rais-
ing money. Olasky writes, "Telethons and jogathons became the most
dramatic private charitable activities: stars would appear on television for
twenty-four hours at a stretch, or long-distance runners would run at so
much per mile, to raise money to pay professionals to help the needy."[17]
He continues, "'Bonding' [with a poor person or family] was reduced to
donors receiving photographs of grateful clients."[18]

THE OXYMORON OF ATHEISTIC COMPASSION

STUDY GUIDE
SESSION 9

"Atheistic compassion" is an oxymoron because atheism provides no
basis for compassion and social justice. That is not to say atheists are never
compassionate; they often are. But their compassion is not driven by their
philosophy and often stands in contradiction to it. The natural ends of
atheistic thought are social Darwinism, survival of the fittest, and selfish
cruelty. Like adherents to many other thought systems, atheists live on
borrowed capital from the biblical worldview. Ironically, atheists' compassion is a function of their humanity in the image of God. In spite of
what their belief system tells them, they care about others because they
were created by a loving God to reflect him.

We have already discussed the ways the atheist/secularist worldview
has shifted the view and practice of compassion. We now consider three
further shifts caused by this worldview: the locus of responsibility, the
prevailing social philosophy, and the economic theory.

Locus of Responsibility: From Voluntary to Professional

At one time citizens helped their suffering neighbors, either working
individually or in the context of private voluntary organizations. Much,
though not all, of this dynamic of personal and voluntary acts of compassion has been pushed off to professional services. The former brings
people together; the latter separates people.

Private voluntary organizations (PVOs, also known as nongovernmental organizations, or NGOs) are what the French historian and social

commentator Alexis de Tocqueville (1805–59) called voluntary associations. He writes in *Democracy in America* that in these organizations love propelled neighbors to help neighbors: "The love and respect of your neighbors must be gained by a long series of small services, hidden deeds of goodness, a persistent habit of kindness, and an established reputation of selflessness. . . . I have seen Americans making great and sincere sacrifices for the key common good and a hundred times I have noticed that, when need be, they almost always gave each other faithful support."[19]

Tocqueville describes how people moved from helping as individuals to increasing leverage through the formation of voluntary associations. "Americans group together to hold fêtes, found seminaries, build inns, construct churches, distribute books, dispatch missionaries to the antipodes. They establish hospitals, prisons, schools by the same method. Finally, if they wish to highlight a truth or develop an opinion by the encouragement of a great example, they form an association."[20]

Tocqueville observed that when the French looked to solve problems, they turned to the state. The British turned to the aristocracy. The Americans, uniquely, turned to one another in the form of voluntary associations.

Over time, volunteers have been replaced by professionals.[21] Many voluntary associations have become quasi-governmental service arms. Community voluntary associations have given way to the new NGO model: large nonprofit organizations employing skilled fund-raisers who acquire money and hire professional staff to care for the poor. In recent years these organizations have largely become contractors for government "charity." World Vision, World Relief, Catholic Social Services, C.A.R.E., Food for the Hungry, and other large nonprofits are funded by government grants as Washington outsources many of the charitable activities it had appropriated for itself. Himmelfarb describes this process as "telescopic philanthropy."[22] The dynamic of personal, relational service of those nearby has largely disappeared. Now, willing helpers are separated by distance and bureaucracy from those they want to help.[23]

In "Response and Recovery after the Joplin Tornado: Lessons Applied and Lessons Learned," Daniel J. Smith and Daniel Sutter write:

On May 22, 2011, a supercell thunderstorm spawned a tornado just east of the Missouri–Kansas state line that rapidly intensified to produce EF-5 damage as it tore a half-mile to three-quarter-mile-wide path of near total destruction across Joplin, Missouri. The death toll in Joplin stands at 161, making this tornado the deadliest in the United States since 1947; no tornado had claimed 100 lives since 1953. The tornado damaged or destroyed an estimated 7,500 homes and more than 500 businesses, with property damage estimated to be $3 billion, the highest ever for a U.S. tornado.

The inept response by federal, state, and local governments to Hurricane Katrina in 2005 shocked the nation. The public-sector responses stood in stark contrast to the private-sector responses. Charities, community organizations, businesses, and the voluntary sector provided significant assistance in the wake of the hurricane. Katrina sparked a debate about the proper roles of the public and private sector in disaster response and recovery, and the Joplin tornado provides an additional case study to inform this debate.[24]

A Joplin, Missouri, resident who was in New Orleans during Hurricane Katrina understood that the residents of the two cities lived out two different "cultures," or mindsets. One understood voluntary associations and the power of the private sector. The other was dependent on government to solve its problems and was waiting for that help to come. The Joplin resident said:

> You're going to see something different here [from New Orleans after Katrina] because there's this resilience and this resolve where the people in this community—that we're not waiting for somebody to come do it for us. We're going to get it done, and other people are attracted to that and come alongside to help and make it happen faster.[25]

There are two cultures at work! The first understands both personal and community responsibility and the spirit of volunteerism in solving problems. The second sees the state as responsible for solving the same problems. This culture empowers the state while disempowering the individual and community, and undermining the power of volunteerism.

Social Philosophy: From Max Weber to Karl Marx

Change in the accepted social philosophy emerged as another influence on the practice of compassion. This is especially seen in two disparate representatives, both of them German: Max Weber and Karl Marx. Weber was a child of a German Reformation family. Believing that ideas have consequences, he attributed the economic development in northern Europe to the Protestant work ethic. He believed that political and economic freedom empowered people to establish societies that created wealth for the sake of the common good. Karl Marx, on the other hand, was a materialist. He believed that matter is all that matters and that economic problems and conditions can be solved only by material means. Accordingly, the solution to poverty is the redistribution of scarce resources. The state becomes the arbiter of economic outcomes, by coercion and force if necessary. From an open-system worldview like Weber's, we get social justice springing from personal compassion and responsibility. People who are poor are empowered to create (and enabled to share) wealth. From a closed-system view like Marx's have come socialistic government welfare programs.

Economic Theory: From Adam Smith to Thomas Malthus

Economic theory is a very powerful influence in the discussion of social justice. This arena experienced a shift from the ideas of Adam Smith (1723–90) to those of Thomas Malthus (1766–1834). Smith believed in a positive-sum economic system that included the human creation of wealth as part of the cultural mandate in the book of Genesis. Malthus, on the other hand, espoused a zero-sum economic system. In this view, resources are by nature material things and by definition limited.

Smith, who was part of the Scottish Enlightenment, is often cited as the father of modern economics and capitalism. His book *The Wealth of Nations* is the first modern work of economics. Although Smith considered himself a deist, his economic thinking reflected the views of the theistic Scottish Puritans. According to Gary Haugen, the Puritan influence is what later led to compassion in American society, which was built on "the Puritans' basic confidence that the world could be constrained and re-formed in accordance with God's revealed will," and fueled by their "demand for holiness, [and their] calling for socially relevant Christian commitment as the proper sequel to conversion."[26]

The Protestant Reformers believed that the universe has a moral dimension. They also regarded creation as an open system. God made humans in his image to work and to steward creation, making it bountiful. Humanity has a moral responsibility for the care of creation and of fellow human beings. From this sense of responsibility came the concept of wealth creation. In Geneva, the "City on the Hill," John Calvin laid the foundations for the economic revolution that birthed a new idea: the middle class. These ideas would spread from Geneva to the English and Scottish Puritans and then to the Puritan founders of the United States.[27]

It was the giants of the Reformation who laid the intellectual foundations for free enterprise and its corollary, private property. But the legacy of atheism is welfare. A world without God has no ultimate ground for hope.

Thomas Malthus was a British social theorist and demographer. In 1798 he published *An Essay on the Principles of Population*. Malthus predicted mass starvation because the rate of food production would be steadily outstripped by population growth. In his essay, he said:

> The power of population is indefinitely greater than the power in the earth to produce subsistence for man. Population, when unchecked, increases in a geometrical ratio. Subsistence increases only in an arithmetical ratio. A slight acquaintance with numbers will shew the immensity of the first power in comparison of the second.[28]

Over two hundred years later, it seems safe to observe that Malthus missed his prediction, largely because his assumptions were wrong (although plenty of Malthusians would vehemently disagree and say he was just way ahead of his time). Malthus was a professing deist. In his view, God was remote and largely irrelevant to daily life. In fact, Malthus's thinking actually reflected the atheistic-materialistic ideas which would soon emerge in the public discussion.

Malthus's ideas still hold sway over modern political and economic theory. Malthusian thinking drives one side in the battle for the soul of the West. Simply put, Malthus argued that human beings breed like rabbits. He called for strictly enforced population controls. Otherwise, too many mouths to feed would overrun too little food. In his thinking, resources are essentially fixed (per the closed-system economic model). The solution is to reduce the world's population by any means necessary. At the same time, Malthus wanted to redistribute scarce resources.

Gertrude Himmelfarb helpfully describes the shift from Adam Smith to Thomas Malthus:

> For Smith, man was a rational being capable of making rational decisions in his own interest; but he was rational because he was a moral and a social being, incorporating in himself the principle of "sympathy" that made him respect the interests of his fellow men as he respected his own interests. By the same token, society was rational and moral. This was implicit in the idea of the "invisible hand," the assumption that the free marketplace, operating naturally and without the intervention of any external force, made the interests of the individual congruent with the general interest.
>
> By pursuing his own interest he [the individual] frequently promotes that of society more effectually than when he really intends to promote it. The same free and natural process ensured the progressive growth of the economy, and this, in turn, brought about the progressive improvement of the lower classes. Thus the interests of the individual were compatible with those of society and the exigencies of economics with the imperatives of morality.

It was Smith's successors, Malthus and Ricardo, who broke the link between individual interest and the general interest, between the wealth of the nation and the welfare of the lower classes—and thus between moral philosophy and political economy. It was they who transformed "economic man" into amoral man (immoral man, their critics charged), and in the process transformed an "optimistic" political economy into a profoundly "pessimistic" one. Where Smith (like Marshall) saw the growth of the population as the precondition for a "progressive" economy and thus the increasing affluence of the entire population, including the poor, Malthus saw it as the inevitable, even fatal, limitation on progress, with especially baneful consequences for the poor.[29]

The influence of Malthusian materialism meant a switch in three related ideas:

1. From free markets to welfare states
2. From seeing the creation as abundance (positive sum) to seeing it as scarcity (zero sum)
3. From creating wealth to redistributing wealth

Judeo-Christian theism gave birth to free markets. Atheistic materialism resulted in welfare states. The path from theism to materialism is a descent from abundance to scarcity. In the former framework, people use their God-given resources, both internal and external, to create wealth. (In chapter 2 we noted the example of Apple founders Steve Jobs and Steve Wozniak, who created more than 500,000 jobs in the Unites States alone.) This is true quite apart from any expressed religious affiliation or belief. It springs naturally from the Judeo-Christian worldview.

As we've discussed, the materialistic framework is built on a closed-system economic model. Wealth is not a product of human imagination but rather is defined as fixed assets in the ground. This mindset creates policies of redistributing "scarce" wealth. We have seen these policies in the welfare states of Europe for two or three generations. We are now seeing them increasingly in the United States and Canada.

As the paradigm in the West has shifted from theism to atheism, society has moved from optimism to pessimism, from hopefulness to hopelessness. As Himmelfarb writes: "The poor were not only pauperized; they were 'de-moralized,' deprived of their moral status as individuals and as members of society. And political economy was similarly 'de-moralized,' divorced from moral philosophy."[30]

How can we reverse this shift from optimism to pessimism, from viewing other human beings with pity rather than acting in compassion? This is the subject of the next chapter.

PART 2

REDEFINING SOCIAL JUSTICE
IN TERMS OF COMPASSION

CHAPTER 5

RADICAL SOCIAL JUSTICE: THE BIBLICAL IMPERATIVE

ompassion, we have seen, doesn't mean what it used to. Not in Western cultures, at least. About 150 years ago *compassion* was used as a
verb: "to compassionate, i.e., to join with in passion." Today *compassion*
is only a noun. In common use it has been reduced to an emotion, a synonym for pity. As the meaning of the word changed, so did the practice.
At one time people suffered together with the poor. Today we feel guilty
and write checks. This change in our concept of compassion has dissolved
our practice of social justice.

True social justice is rooted in the heart of God, who is the source
of compassion. It follows that nothing about the essence of social justice
has changed. Rather, as Western society has abandoned biblical thinking,
our ideas and practices about social justice have eroded. The solution for
reversing that erosion lies in the same resource: the revelation of God.

We now examine the biblical understandings of social justice. A
return to biblical terminology—to compassion and concepts related to
it—will bear fruit in a biblical practice. God himself is the author of compassion. Therefore, if we are serious about compassion, we must understand God's view of it as revealed in the Bible.

BIBLICAL COMPASSION

In this section we will examine the Old Testament and New Testament terms behind our English word *compassion*.[1] Our choice of words has a profound effect on our own lives and on the society around us. Much of our language today has been shaped by the atheist-materialist worldview. Christians need to go back to God's self-disclosure about his own nature. He is compassion!

A study of the biblical words translated "compassion" reveals three key ideas. First, compassion springs from the heart of God. God describes himself to humans as "the LORD, the LORD, the compassionate and gracious God, slow to anger, abounding in love and faithfulness" (Exod. 34:6). Without God's intervention, the world would not know compassion, only the Darwinian animal nature of cruelty—"red in tooth and claw."

Second, compassion manifests itself in God's steadfast love and in the incarnation of Jesus Christ. This is seen in Christ's suffering together with us and for our salvation.

Third, compassion is to be the hallmark of God's people. Social justice is not an afterthought of the Christian life. It is the forethought. Christians are to be unique people, participating in Christ's suffering, drawing alongside the broken and bleeding in their communities, and suffering together with them. We do this by sharing our whole lives—our time, talents, and treasure.

Chamal

The Hebrew word *chamal*, used forty-five times in the Old Testament, is one example of the biblical words translated "compassion." The word appears in the story of Moses's birth. Pharaoh was fearful of the growing number of Hebrew slaves. To stem the Hebrew tide, he ordered their midwives to kill all newborn Hebrew boys. But the midwives feared God more than they feared Pharaoh, and they often hid the male infants.

When Moses was born, his mother hid him for three months. She then put him in a papyrus basket and set him in the reeds along the bank of the Nile. In God's providence, "the daughter of Pharaoh came down to bathe at the river. And her maidens walked along the riverside; and when she saw the ark among the reeds, she sent her maid to get it. And when she opened it, she saw the child, and behold, the baby wept. So she had compassion [*chamal*] on him, and said, 'This is one of the Hebrews' children'" (Exod. 2:5–6 NKJV). Pharaoh's daughter did not simply feel sorry for this Hebrew baby whom Pharaoh had condemned to death. She acted, risking her own well-being in order to have compassion on the baby Moses. She showed mercy.

The same is true of the "righteous Gentiles," a term used by Holocaust survivors to describe non-Jews who risked their lives to save Jews by sheltering them in their homes during World War II. Sometimes this genuine compassion cost them their lives in Hitler's death camps.

A lesser-known example of biblical compassion is that of Paul Rusesabagina, manager of the Hôtel des Mille Collines in Kigali, Rwanda. Rusesabagina provided shelter and protection for 1,268 Hutu and Tutsi refugees to keep them from being killed by the Interahamwe militia ravaging Rwanda. His story is told in the movie *Hotel Rwanda*.

These are examples of *chamal* writ large. Millions of smaller acts of mercy take place all around the world every day.

Rahamîm and Related Words

The Hebrew *rahamîm* is used of God in two striking pictures. The Bible compares God's love to the love of a mother and of a father.

> Can a mother forget the baby at her breast and have no compassion [*rahamîm*] on the child she has borne? Though she may forget, I will not forget you! (Isa. 49:15)

> As a father has compassion on his children, so the LORD has *compassion* [*rahamîm*] on those who fear him. (Ps. 103:13)

In both cases the compassion of the parent finds its archetype in the compassion of God. Maternal love comes from the heart of God. Likewise, a father loves his children because of who God is. Compassion is one of God's attributes that is to flow from God's children.

One of the most powerful accounts of maternal love in the Bible is the story recorded in 1 Kings 3:16–28. Two prostitutes come to Solomon to contend over a baby they both claim as their own. Solomon's legendary wisdom leads him to offer a solution: "Cut the living child in two, and give half to one and half to the other" (1 Kings 3:25). Because of the power of maternal love, Solomon's ruse works perfectly. The real mother immediately responds, "Please, my lord, give her the living baby! Don't kill him!" (3:26). Although the Bible never calls God a mother, maternal love is clearly part of the stamp of God's image on woman. God is the author of motherhood as well as fatherhood.[2]

The Hebrew term *rahamîm* is part of a family of words with further nuances important to an understanding of compassion. One term, *rechem*, is translated in Job 24:20 (NASB) as "mother" (i.e., "the female who carries a child to birth, implying care and concern for the child"[3]). The heart of the word is revealed in that it is translated "womb" twenty-one times. A related word, *racham*, likewise is translated "womb," thus continuing the powerful picture of compassion as womb love. When God designed the woman, he sculpted a place in her body known as "compassion." In Genesis 49:25, referring to Joseph's protection by God, God affirms that the blessings of heaven are found in the breast and the womb:

> . . . because of your father's God, who helps you,
>   because of the Almighty who blesses you
> with blessings of skies above,
>   blessings of the deep springs below,
>   blessings of the breast and the womb.

How fascinating that the root of this family of words, which comprise the very character of God, is *womb*! At the same time, how grievous that the womb, created as the very picture of compassion, has become a place of death. Every day for the past forty years, 110,000 places of compassion have been violated; every year, globally, forty million precious unborn lives are destroyed.[4]

A third related word, *rachum*, translated "compassionate," is used of God himself. As we have seen before, Exodus 34:6–7 refers to God as "the LORD, the compassionate and gracious God, slow to anger, abounding in love and faithfulness, maintaining love to thousands, and forgiving wickedness, rebellion and sin." The reluctant prophet Jonah pushed back against this merciful and compassionate God. With unmistakable irony, the narrator records this discouraged man of God complaining when he finds God too compassionate for his liking.

> When God saw what they [the Ninevites] did and how they turned from their evil ways, he relented and did not bring on them the destruction he had threatened. But to Jonah this seemed very wrong, and he became angry. He prayed to the LORD, "Isn't this what I said, LORD, when I was still at home? That is what I tried to forestall by fleeing to Tarshish. I knew that you are a gracious and compassionate God, slow to anger and abounding in love, a God who relents from sending calamity." (Jon. 3:10–4:2)

Jonah is so angry that he asks God to take away his life. God patiently replies, "Is it right for you to be angry?" and attempts to show Jonah the meaning of compassion through an object lesson. He then reiterates his compassion for the people of Nineveh.

Oiktirmos

The Greek noun *oiktirmos* means "mercy" or "compassion." Paul uses this word when he writes, "For [God] says to Moses, 'I will have mercy on whom I have mercy, and I will have compassion [*oiktiro*] on whom I have compassion'" (Rom. 9:15). God is merciful. Mercy flows from his being. He deeply loves those whom he created, even in their rebellion.

Mercy originates in God, and it is to show up in us: "Therefore, as God's chosen people, holy and dearly loved, clothe yourselves with compassion [*oiktirmos*], kindness, humility, gentleness, and patience" (Col. 3:12). God's people are to exhibit mercy. Our acts of compassion are reflections of him.

Chesed and Eleos

Another pair of terms from the Old Testament and the New Testament are *chesed* (Hebrew) and *eleos* (Greek). The Hebrew noun *chesed* means loyal love, unfailing kindness, devotion. "*Chesed* . . . is the basis of God's whole relationship to man."[5] We see this in Psalm 63:3: "Because your love is better than life, my lips will glorify you." God's outgoing love is not capricious, not the unpredictable mood of a fickle, lesser god. Rather, it is "something on which men can absolutely depend because it is founded on the fidelity and steadfastness of God to himself and to his promises."[6]

One of the most poetic lines of the Psalms is "Love [*chesed*] and faithfulness meet together; righteousness and peace kiss each other" (Ps. 85:10).

Chesed is to be characteristic of human relationships: "He has shown you, O mortal, what is good. And what does the LORD require of you? To act justly and to love mercy [*chesed*] and to walk humbly with your God" (Mic. 6:8). The book of Joshua records Rahab's kindness to the spies in a potentially costly way: "Now then, please swear to me by the LORD that you will show kindness [*chesed*] to my family, because I have shown kindness [*chesed*] to you. Give me a sure sign that you will spare the lives of my father and mother, my brothers and sisters, and all who belong to them—and that you will save us from death" (Josh. 2:12–13).

The New Testament uses the word *eleos*, the Greek equivalent to *chesed*. The merciful heart of God was manifest in the incarnation of Christ. We read of God's mercy in Mary's song, a response to the angel's announcement of Jesus's birth: "[God's] mercy [*eleos*] extends to those who fear him, from generation to generation. He has performed mighty deeds with his arm; he has scattered those who are proud in their inmost thoughts. He has brought down rulers from their thrones but has lifted up the humble. He has filled the hungry with good things but has sent the rich away empty" (Luke 1:50–53).

The same affirmation shows up in Zechariah's prophecy a few verses later. God has visited his people "to show mercy [*eleos*] to our ancestors and to remember his holy covenant, the oath he swore to our father

Abraham, to rescue us from the hand of our enemies, and to enable us to serve him without fear in holiness and righteousness before him all our days" (Luke 1:72–75).

We see divine mercy further breaking into the reality of human misery during Jesus's ministry: "When [the blind man] heard that it was Jesus of Nazareth, he began to shout, 'Jesus, Son of David, have mercy [*eleeo*] on me!' Many rebuked him and told him to be quiet, but he shouted all the more, 'Son of David, have mercy on me!'" (Mark 10:47–48). Jesus, who is God incarnate, is the truest image of mercy that we have.

Both the Old and New Testaments make it clear that those who follow God must also display his mercy. The parable of the good Samaritan (Luke 10:25–37), which we looked at in chapter 3, revolves around the word *eleos*. Jesus tells this parable to a Jewish lawyer who is trying to avoid responsibility for helping the poor. At the end of the story, Jesus asks the lawyer, "Which of these three do you think was a neighbor to the man who fell into the hands of robbers?" The man replies, "The one who had mercy [*eleos*] on him." Jesus then tells him, "Go and do likewise" (Luke 10:36–37).

This is an imperative for us: *Go and do likewise*. God's mercy, whatever the word used for it, should characterize the Christian's life. Followers of Christ, who have received mercy themselves, are to manifest God's compassion by actively showing mercy and kindness to people in their deepest needs. This is not social justice from a distance. This is not a collective practice of social justice. This is social justice at its most basic: human being to human being.

A COMPASSIONATE CHRIST

STUDY GUIDE
SESSION 11

Let's consider two further New Testament families of words translated "compassion." The first refers to the compassion of Christ; the second to suffering servanthood.

The first family of Greek words, from the verb *splagchnizomai*, "to be moved, to have compassion," characterizes the compassion of Christ. The

Gospel writers tell the story of a man with a dreaded skin disease who approached Jesus. The man said in bold belief, "If you are willing, you can make me clean" (Mark 1:40). "I am willing," Jesus said. And he did more than speak. He healed. And note *how* he did it. At other times Jesus had healed with words only (Luke 5:24–25). He had also healed from a distance (Luke 7:1–10). Yet compassion for this social outcast, the leper whose condition isolated him from the community, moved Jesus to go beyond what was necessary. The scripture says, "Then Jesus, moved with compassion, stretched out *His* hand and touched him, and said to him, "I am willing; be cleansed" (Mark 1:41 NKJV). Jesus's compassion drove him to touch the "untouchable."

Three parables also tell the story of God's unlimited compassion bound up in the person of Jesus.

- The unforgiving servant (Matt. 18:23–35): "The servant therefore fell down before him, saying, 'Master, have patience with me, and I will pay you all.' Then the master of that servant was moved with compassion [*splagchnizomai*], released him, and forgave him the debt" (vv. 26–27 NKJV).
- The prodigal son (Luke 15:11–32): "So he got up and went to his father. But while he was still a long way off, his father saw him and was filled with compassion [*splagchnizomai*] for him; he ran to his son, threw his arms around him and kissed him" (v. 20).
- The good Samaritan (Luke 10:30–37): "But a certain Samaritan, as he journeyed, came where he was. And when he saw him, he had compassion [*splagchnizomai*]" (v. 33 NKJV).

How is the compassion of Christ seen today? In the lives of his followers. "If anyone has material possessions and sees a brother or sister in need but has no pity on them, how can the love of God be in that person?" (1 John 3:17).

COMPASSION MEANS SERVANTS WHO SUFFER

The second family of words includes and derives from the term *pascho*. We find this word family primarily in the Synoptic Gospels (Matthew, Mark, and Luke), Acts, and Hebrews, where it relates to the nature of suffering servants. This compassion describes both the suffering of Christ and the cost to Christians who follow him. Once again, we see that compassion means joining another's passion to suffer with him or her.

The Bible declares Jesus as the ultimate suffering Servant. He suffered (*pascho*):

- As atonement for our sins: "And so Jesus also suffered outside the city gate to make the people holy through his own blood" (Heb. 13:12).
- To empathize with our afflictions: "For we do not have a high priest who is unable to empathize with our weaknesses, but we have one who has been tempted in every way, just as we are—yet he did not sin" (Heb. 4:15).
- As an example for us: "To this you were called, because Christ suffered for you, leaving you an example, that you should follow in his steps" (1 Pet. 2:21).

Note also that Jesus did not suffer for "our deliverance *from* earthly suffering, but [for our] deliverance *for* earthly suffering."[7]

Since the children have flesh and blood, he too shared in their humanity so that by his death he might break the power of him who holds the power of death—that is, the devil— and free those who all their lives were held in slavery by their fear of death. For surely it is not angels he helps, but Abraham's descendants. For this reason he had to be made like them, fully human in every way, in order that he might become a merciful and faithful high priest in service to God, and that he might make atonement for the sins

of the people. Because he himself suffered when he was tempted,
he is able to help those who are being tempted. (Heb. 2:14–18)

In contrast to the so-called prosperity gospel, which wants to make
the Christian life free from pain or loss, Jesus calls us to suffering: "Who-
ever wants to be my disciple must deny themselves and take up their cross
daily and follow me" (Luke 9:23).

Today the church is marked by a theology of comfort. Christ calls us
to live out a theology of suffering, to be free to suffer together with others.

Suffering and fellowship go hand in hand. We witness the radical call
of the cross in Philippians 1:29: "For it has been granted to you on behalf
of Christ not only to believe him, but also to suffer for him." And again
in 1 Peter 4:12–13: "Dear friends, do not be surprised at the fiery ordeal
that has come on you to test you, as though something strange were hap-
pening to you. But rejoice inasmuch as you participate in the sufferings of
Christ, so that you may be overjoyed when his glory is revealed."

A Christian's suffering is not an indication that something is wrong.
Suffering is a normal part of the Christian life as we identify with a broken
world and come alongside those who are bleeding, just as Christ did in
his day.

The world which Christ entered was filled with brokenness and suffering. William Barclay, in his book *The Beatitudes and the Lord's Prayer for
Everyman*, demonstrates the cruelty and hardness of heart that was common in the time and place into which Jesus was born. He cites numerous
ancient sources, which are worth repeating here.

The Jew was merciless to the sinner and merciless to the Gentile. . . . According to the Law it was forbidden to help a Gentile
mother and her child even in the crisis of childbirth. If a Jew
had become a renegade from the faith, it was not even lawful to
summon medical attention for him, even if his life was in dan-
ger. The Gentiles were to be killed as snakes are crushed; they
were created for no other purpose than to be fuel for the fires
of Hell.[8]

In the Roman world life was merciless, especially to the slave and to the child. The slave, as Aristotle said (*Nicomachean Ethics* 8.II.6), was no different from a living tool, and what consideration can a tool receive? A master could, and did, kill his slave, as when Vedius Pollio flung his slave to the savage lampreys in the fish pool of his courtyard, because he had stumbled and broken a goblet (Pliny, *Natural History* 9.23).[9]

Cato's advice when he writes on agriculture: "When you take possession of a farm, look over the livestock and hold a sale. Sell your oil, if the price is satisfactory, and sell the surplus of your wine and grain. Sell worn-out oxen, blemished cattle and sheep, wool, hides, an old wagon, old tools, an old slave, a sickly slave, and whatever else is superfluous" (*On Agriculture* 2.7).[10]

The ancient world practiced the exposure of children. The unwanted child was simply thrown out like refuse. Hilarion writes to his wife Alis in 1 BC with the strangest mixture of love and callousness: "Hilarion to his wife Alis, warmest greetings. . . . I want you to know that we are still in Alexandria. Don't worry if when they all go home, I stay on in Alexandria. I beg and entreat you, take care of the little child; and as soon as we get our pay, I will send it up to you. If—good luck to you!—you bear a child, if it is a boy; let it live; if it is a girl, throw it out. You told Aphrodisias to tell me, 'Don't forget me.' How can I possibly forget you. Don't worry."[11]

The exposure of an unwanted child was normal routine. In Stobacus (*Eclogues* 75) there is a saying: "The poor man raises his sons, but the daughters, if one is poor, we expose."[12]

The child who was weak or sickly or ill-formed had little chance of survival. In the Republic (460B) Plato insists that only the children of better unions must be kept, and any defective child must be done away with. "Let there be a law," says Aristotle, "that no deformed child shall be reared." (*Politics* 7.14.10)[13]

Even Seneca lays it down: "Mad dogs we knock on the head; the fierce and savage ox we slay; sickly sheep we put to the knife to keep them from infecting the flock; unnatural progeny we destroy; we drown even children who at birth are weakly and abnormal. It is not anger but reason which separates the harmful from the sound."[14]

These accounts testify to the brokenness of the human heart, the depth of indifference, the cruelty of a depraved humanity. Into such a world the Savior was born, the One full of compassion and mercy, the suffering Servant. His followers have brought healing and reconciliation to much of the globe, establishing hospitals and schools and laying the basis for modern notions of human rights. Yet we are not without more contemporary examples of the brokenness of societies, the need for Christ's followers to continue his compassionate service. Barclay gives one example: "One of Mary Slessor's most heart-breaking problems in Calabar was the fact that the Africans dreaded twins, as being of evil omen. They were never allowed to live; they were killed, crushed into an earthenware pot, and flung to the leopards to devour."[15]

Today in places like India and Bangladesh, children are deliberately maimed to elicit public sympathy and render them more effective beggars. Children in Thailand who are born with a disability are often abandoned. As Christians we decry such horrors. But do we understand the cost involved to turn the tide? The book of Hebrews indicates that suffering is sometimes necessary for the advancement of the kingdom.

Women received back their dead, raised to life again. There were others who were tortured, refusing to be released so that they might gain an even better resurrection. Some faced jeers and flogging, and even chains and imprisonment. They were put to death by stoning; they were sawed in two; they were killed by the sword. They went about in sheepskins and goatskins, destitute, persecuted and mistreated—the world was not worthy of them. They wandered in deserts and mountains, living in caves and in holes in the ground. These were all commended for their faith, yet none of them received what had been promised, since God had planned something better for us so that only together with us would they be made perfect. (Heb. 11:35–40)

Biblical scholar Walter Brueggemann writes:

Jesus in his solidarity with the marginal ones is *moved to compassion*. Compassion constitutes a radical form of criticism, for it announces that the hurt is to be taken seriously, that the hurt is not to be accepted as normal and natural but is an abnormal and unacceptable condition for humanness. In the arrangement of "lawfulness" in Jesus' time, as in the ancient empire of Pharaoh, the one unpermitted quality of relation was compassion. Empires are never built or maintained on the basis of compassion. The norms of law (social control) are never accommodated to persons, but persons are accommodated to the norms. Otherwise the norms will collapse and with them the whole power arrangement. Thus the compassion of Jesus is to be understood not simply as a personal emotional reaction but as a public criticism in which he dares to act upon his concern against the entire numbness of his social context.[16]

Christ did not die to make us safe. He died so that we, like him, would challenge the world's system. He died to make us dangerous.

CHAPTER 6

PRINCIPLES OF COMPASSION

STUDY GUIDE
SESSION 12

What does applied compassion (another way to say "social justice") look like, as God intends it? From a study of the Bible's terms for compassion, we turn now to the essential matter of applying what we have learned from the Bible about compassion, especially in the realm of social justice. We can do so in confidence that we are God's fellow workers. We are joining with the God of compassion to address his kingdom agenda of social justice.

A world in which Christ had never come would be a pitiless environment. But we do not live in such a world. God has visited our planet. His compassion was manifested most powerfully at Calvary, and it continues to be demonstrated through his people. The brokenness, hunger, and poverty around us create opportunities for us to demonstrate the loving heart of God. For that to happen, our minds must be transformed, as Paul wrote to the Romans: "Do not conform to the pattern of this world, but be transformed by the renewing of your mind. Then you will be able to test and approve what God's will is—his good, pleasing and perfect will" (Rom. 12:2).

Why is a transformed mind necessary to a life of Christian compassion? Because our behaviors are driven by our thinking. Only by beginning at the level of worldview can we accurately analyze the problems of the brokenness in our world. Effective solutions also require a grasp of worldview issues. It would surprise many people to hear that, ultimately, the underlying causes of poverty are moral and metaphysical in nature, not, as most people think, physical and economic. To take the Bible seriously is to recognize the moral and metaphysical causes of poverty and hunger.[1] Here are a few examples of worldviews that lead to poverty and create barriers to development:

- Men are superior to women.
- Work is a curse.
- History is something that happens to you (fatalism).
- The universe is capricious and unknowable.
- Ignorance is a virtue.
- Resources are physical things in the ground.

Yet so much of our response to the plight of people caught in poverty operates without this fundamental understanding. When we fail to recognize this, our attempts to eradicate hunger and alleviate poverty fail. The earlier example of Haiti is just one powerful evidence of this. Once we have this understanding in hand, a biblical worldview informs our behaviors, both at the individual level and the level of society.

When we look at individuals who are poor, we are seeing humans made in the image of God. Thus our doctrine of man is informed by our doctrine of God. That is, how we understand God will drive how we understand humans. Timothy Keller says, "If you are trying to live a life in accordance with the Bible, the concept and call to justice are inescapable. We do justice when we give all human beings their due as creations of God."[2]

Modern thinkers have pushed God from the public square. They have denied God's intervention in human life. This separation of the moral from the material has resulted in faulty approaches to development work and poverty fighting. The foundation of the biblical concept of development is a different moral philosophy. The Greek word that captures this is *oikonomia*, stewardship of a household. The Bible presents humans not as ones who seek their own purposes independently from their Creator, but as stewards with the responsibility to manage the affairs of another—in this case, God.

To recognize God's ownership of the universe is to acknowledge that economic life, as well as religious and spiritual life, matters to God. Thus it is a Christian concern to address poverty and hunger. God did not intend his creation to languish. While the creation's fundamental healing is bound up in the cross (Col. 1:20), God's human agents are to bring healing and hope on his behalf (see, for example, Isa. 1:15–17; 58:6–7). This means that progress in the material world is tied to progress in moral behavior. Today it is considered politically incorrect to talk about "civilizing" people, societies, or nations. There are certainly historical examples of wrong ways to "civilize" people. But because humans' moral nature cannot be separated from our economic responsibilities, a civilizing process is necessary to our prosperity. Without such a conscious process, lawlessness will grow and societies will become more brutal.

We see this in the impoverishment that generally accompanies moral decline. Consider, for example, the state of many inner cities in the United States. A perfect storm of moral decline—absent dads, gang activity, substance abuse, crime—drives stable families and businesses away. As these assets disappear, so do job opportunities. Income levels drop, welfare increases, poverty grows. It could be seen as the opposite of a civilizing process (i.e., building a civil society), a sort of return to the wild.

On the other hand, disciplined behavior lies at the core of public and private life as God intended it. Prosperous and free societies are characterized by a set of virtues that can be captured by the term "Protestant ethic." The elements of this ethic are hard work, thrift, delayed gratification, self-reliance, giving, trustworthiness, a desire for progress, and stewardship of the creation.

Oikonomia, or the Protestant ethic, is fueled by discipline. Discipline seems painful (Heb. 12:11), but it is driven by optimism and hope. God has intervened in our world. In Jesus, he has inaugurated the kingdom. Christ's conquering work at Calvary guarantees the final consummation of that kingdom, and in the interim, leads us forward toward that goal

(Matt. 6:10). Human beings are God's vice-regents over the creation (Gen. 2:15). We partner with the Creator. This is the Bible's view, that cooperation between God and man leads to progress and ultimate success. Contrast that with the man-centered moral philosophy of atheism, which pessimistically assumes "that the growth of population would condemn the lowest class of the poor to a life of 'misery and vice' and doom all of the poor to a perpetual struggle for survival."[3]

From the optimistic perspective of partnering with God to work for social justice, we can now look at specific ways of applying compassion. To do this we have structured this chapter around seven ABCs of compassion as formulated by Marvin Olasky: affiliation, bonding, categorization, discernment, employment, freedom, God.[4]

AFFILIATION

The principle of affiliation in social justice is reflected in the biblical notion of community. As we saw in chapter 1, Thomas Aquinas, Luigi Taparelli, and Pope Leo XIII understood that every person is part of a larger community. Because God is Community (Trinity), to be made in the image of God means to be made for relationships in community. Our health is dependent on the health of the community.

Pastor Gary Skinner of Watoto Church in Kampala, Uganda, is fond of saying, "The problems of the city are the problems of the church."[5] Similarly, the vision of Redeemer Presbyterian Church in New York City, pastored by Timothy Keller, is "to help build a great city for all people through a movement of the gospel."[6] These pastors from different parts of the globe recognize that the church is not an isolated or internally focused institution. The church exists for others. It is present to serve the needs of the community. Although the church as the body of Christ should be leading in community service, the fact is that all human institutions—families, businesses, civic institutions, mosques, synagogues—are responsible to promote political and economic justice in the communities around them.

God's triune nature gives inherent value to the individual and the community. Both are important, and both have responsibility. Humans, God's image-bearing creatures, share some characteristics with the animals but in other ways are distinct from animals. One such distinction is our responsibility to family, community, society, and the world at large. These responsibilities are often trivialized or trampled on by unthinking acts of charity. How many tons of food, how many containers of used clothing have we indiscriminately doled out in America's inner cities and in poor communities in Africa, Asia, and Latin America? When we ignore human responsibilities and simply give aid, we erode important social connections. In the late nineteenth century, Mary Richmond of the Baltimore Organizing Society noted: "Relief given without reference to friends and neighbors is accompanied by moral loss. . . . Poor neighborhoods are doomed to grow poorer and more sordid, whenever the natural ties of neighborliness are weakened by our well-meant but unintelligent interference."[7]

When social justice is reduced to the redistribution of money, all we have to do is cut a check to a charity or pay more taxes. Help is at arm's length and impersonal. *Relational* social justice, by contrast, demands that individuals (as well as families, businesses, and civic and religious institutions) get involved with people. It requires giving of our time and talents in addition to our treasure to nurture fellow humans and contribute to their flourishing. Giving money is easier but less effective than getting involved. Perhaps the former is so popular because it is more about the giver's guilt reduction than it is about the receiver's benefit and progress.

Those involved in serving people in need must ask, "How can we reinforce affiliation?" Affiliation occurs at multiple levels, from very personal to less personal. The most personal and foundational affiliation is immediate family, which is followed by extended family, then mediating structures like churches and civic organizations, then private charitable organizations (such as the International Red Cross), then government (first local, then state, then federal). As we ascend the list, solutions become more impersonal and disaffiliation—the breakup of support structures such as families—becomes more certain. The federal government, often seen as the first line of defense, should actually be the last resort. When we are confronted with a material need, it's considered normal today to look for some government program. We should, however, look first to the family. When we encounter someone who needs help, we should ask, "How can I help reaffiliate this needy person with his or her family?" If immediate family is not there or able to help, then look to the extended family, then to the church or a civic organization. Poverty is almost never solved by government efforts.

One of the greatest causes of poverty is disaffiliation, separation of families and communities. Spouses divorce. Men abandon their families. Absent fathers neglect child payments. Children run away from home. One hundred fifty years ago, poverty workers regarded affiliation as being of first priority. They recognized the need to understand the individual. Who is their family? What religious group do they belong to? What club are they a member of? The first line of defense against poverty was to restore people's affiliations.

Today, practices by the "poverty industry" disaffiliate poor people. When welfare programs reward single women for having children, they are discouraging marriage, thus destroying affiliation. Child sponsorship programs that give directly to the child shred the father's role as bread-winner. The child looks to the nongovernmental organization rather than a parent for his or her resources. This is disaffiliation at the family level. Here's an example of disaffiliation at the level of local economies: bundles of food and goods from abroad that often put local merchants and farmers out of business.

In the Old Testament, social justice is known as *shalom*—peace, wholeness, prosperity. This peace, the framework for justice, was bought at an exorbitant cost through the cross of Christ. God has justified us by grace and calls us to live justly. This is to be done in our internal and our external worlds. Just as holiness is a personal spiritual discipline, justice is a public spiritual discipline. Justice means right relationships, or affiliations, with God, with our fellow citizens, and with creation.

BONDING

The second principle is bonding. When reaffiliation is impossible, bonding must occur. New relationships must be built. The apostle John pictures the ultimate bonding: "The Word became flesh and made his dwelling among us" (John 1:14). Christ's incarnation is the ultimate manifestation of God's compassion. To become incarnate, Christ had to leave heaven and eternity to live among us. Jesus gave the final word on relationship, on "suffering together with."

Social reformer Jacob Riis wrote in 1890 about the value of giving people opportunities to see how the "other half" lives: "The poor and the well-to-do have been brought closer together, in an every-day companionship that cannot but be productive of the best results, to the one who gives no less than to the one who receives."[8]

Charities need to build bridges, not barriers, between those who serve and those in need. The Big Brothers Big Sisters program serves as a good example of bonding. Volunteers become "big brothers" or "big sisters" to children who are struggling, often without a mother or father. The volunteers come alongside children and build relationships with them, and bonding results. Another example of bonding is the Hunger Corps program within Food for the Hungry (FH). Hunger Corps teams go into villages and communities in developing countries to live there, build relationships, and bond with the people. The scale is small and personal rather than large and impersonal. FH founder Larry Ward used to say, "They die one at a time. You can help them one at a time." This is life-on-life relationship building.

Timothy Keller emphasizes the importance of relationships in God's view of righteousness.

> Bible scholar Alec Motyer defines "righteous" as those "right with God and therefore committed to putting right all other relationships in life." This means, then, that Biblical righteousness is inevitably "social," because it is about relationships. When most modern people see the word "righteousness" in the Bible, they tend to

think of it in terms of private morality, such as sexual chastity or diligence in prayer and Bible study. But in the Bible *tzadeqah* refers to day-to-day living in which a person conducts *all* relationships in family and society with fairness, generosity, and equity.[9]

In other words, someone of unimpeachable private piety who is regarded by others as unkind, aloof, or selfish would not be seen as righteous by God. Righteousness has both a public and a private expression.

A Chinese proverb captures this truth well: "Go to the people. Live with them. Learn from them. Love them. Start with what they know. Build with what they have. But with the best leaders, when the work is done, the task accomplished, the people will say, 'We have done this ourselves.'" How does that occur? By this process of bonding, in which people's lives begin to touch each other's in new and dynamic ways. For the Christ follower, it means that where there is no network, we must become the family. This is biblical servanthood played out in real life, a picture of social justice shaped by God's own heart.

CATEGORIZATION

Olasky's third principle of social justice is categorization. This term is used to capture an important, if politically incorrect, aspect of biblical compassion: it discriminates. It's easy to lose sight of the justice in "social justice." But Yahweh is a God of mercy *and* justice. True compassion is both warm-hearted and clear-headed. This relationship between love and discipline, sometimes called "tough love," is right out of the Bible.

Give proper recognition to those widows who are really in need. But if a widow has children or grandchildren, these should learn first of all to put their religion into practice by caring for their own family and so repaying their parents and grandparents, for this is pleasing to God. The widow who is really in need and left all alone puts her hope in God and continues night and day to pray and to ask God for help. But the widow who lives for pleasure is dead even while she lives. Give the people these instructions, so that no one may be open to blame. Anyone who does not provide for their relatives, and especially for their own household, has denied the faith and is worse than an unbeliever. (1 Tim. 5:3–8)

Notice the three categories of widows. Those with extended family are to be cared for by their offspring. Those identified as "truly widows" (translated "really in need" in the NIV) have no extended family. These are the responsibility of the church. The third category are self-indulgent widows (in the NIV, "the widow who lives for pleasure"). The Greek term translated "lives for pleasure" means "to indulge oneself excessively in satisfying one's own appetites and desires."[10] This group is to receive no help from the church.

At one time, people who worked in the arena of compassion practiced categorization. That is, they distinguished between two kinds of poverty: the deserving poor and the undeserving poor. Today, we have lost these important distinctions. We have created impersonal institutions in which these differences have dissolved. As a result, we put everybody, without distinction, in one category, "the poor," and everyone in that category is deserving of our unending aid. This lumping of all people who are poor into one category breeds corruption, injustice, and ever-growing welfare programs. The Bible categorizes people who are poor as either *deserving* or *undeserving* (even using the phrase "undeserving poor" seems an anathema to the modern mind). Within the category of deserving poor, the Bible further distinguishes the *widows and orphans* and the *laboring poor*. These biblical concepts framed the service of compassion workers in previous generations who consciously functioned from a biblical worldview. Where there is no categorization, all poor people, by definition, are deserving of our aid.

Let's look at the two main kinds of poverty—the deserving poor (including the laboring poor) and undeserving poor—and observe how they were dealt with in the past and how they can be dealt with compassionately today.

The deserving poor—that is, those who deserve to receive unconditional help—include orphans, the elderly, the incurably ill, accident victims, and so on. A subgroup of the deserving poor is the laboring poor, which we address separately below.

James makes clear that true religion is not "religious" at all (in today's common understanding of that term). He writes: "Religion that God our Father accepts as pure and faultless is this: to look after orphans and widows in their distress and to keep oneself from being polluted by the world" (James 1:27). True religion is caring for the vulnerable. Jesus makes this point when he creates an image of his return at the end of time. He will come back as a king, and from his throne he will separate the sheep, those who cared for the needy and vulnerable, from the goats, those who did not care for the poor (Matt. 25:31–46).

Here's another example of categorization in the Bible. Timothy makes a distinction between a "widow indeed"—someone who has no means of support and the "wanton widow"—one who gives herself to self-indulgence (1 Tim. 5:3–6). The one is vulnerable and to be cared for; the other is to be left to her own devices. It is both a personal and communal responsibility to care for the truly vulnerable, the widows and the orphans. In the past, such people were served freely. Some were welcomed into the homes of others to live as part of the household. Or if housing wasn't the need, poverty workers would visit and care for them in other ways. God has a special place in his heart for people whose circumstances leave them highly vulnerable. Keller writes:

> If you look at every place the word [*mishpat*] is used in the Old Testament, several classes of persons continually come up. Over and over again, *mishpat* describes taking up the care and cause of widows, orphans, immigrants, and the poor—those who have been called "the quartet of the vulnerable." . . . Today this quartet would be expanded to include the refugee, the migrant worker, the homeless, and many single parents and elderly people.[11]

Our profession as followers of Christ means that we must be quick to respond to the needs of the most vulnerable. This applies to both those around us and those far away. In his book *The Hole in Our Gospel*, Richard Stearns, president of World Vision United States, suggests that needy fellow humans, whether near or far away, must not be brushed aside as if their lives do not matter.

> If we are honest with ourselves, we must admit that we simply have less empathy for people of other cultures living in faraway countries than we do for Americans. Our compassion for others seems to be directly correlated to whether people are close to us socially, emotionally, culturally, ethnically, economically, and geographically. But why do we distinguish the value of one human life from another? Why is it so easy to shut out the cries of these dying foreign children from our ears?[12]

Indeed, we must not overlook the cries of the most needy and vulnerable in society, wherever they are.

A subset of the deserving poor are the laboring poor, people who are able and willing to work but who lack opportunity for employment. These people are hardworking, industrious, and persistent. They do not need a handout; they need a hand up. They need an opportunity to work. The classic biblical illustration is found in the book of Ruth. In this dramatic story, we read that Ruth had lost the breadwinners in her family to starvation. She was impoverished and starving herself. Boaz, a wealthy landowner and farmer, provided her with immediate food from his own table then gave her an opportunity to work to provide for her own needs and the needs of her mother-in-law, Naomi (for this remarkable story read Ruth 2).

In the case of the laboring poor, individuals, businesses, and communities are to provide opportunity for these people who are able and willing to work. The point is that many people are poor in spite of their efforts to earn a living. They are to be distinguished from those who are the undeserving poor.

The second main category is the undeserving poor, those who are *able but unwilling to work.* For these it is not a matter of ability but of attitude. These people may be lazy, averse to work, or idle. They may be substance abusers, criminals, or intemperate, shiftless, or antisocial people. These folks may be proud and think that physical work, or a particular type of work like dishwashing or digging ditches, is beneath them. Often they have a victim mentality and believe that society owes them a living.

The book of Proverbs speaks repeatedly of those able and unwilling to work: "The craving of a sluggard will be the death of him, because his hands refuse to work" (Prov. 21:25). The lesson of the ant in Proverbs 6:6–11 is intended for those able and not willing to work. The consequence of indolence is severe: "Poverty will come on you like a thief."

In previous generations, people working among the poor distinguished between the laboring and undeserving poor by offering employment to those able to work. When someone applied for charity, he or she would be asked to chop wood or sew garments. The fuel and clothing of the laboring poor would then be made available to the widow and the orphan. Those who agreed to chop or sew received dignity by working and were given further opportunity to work.[13] Those *unwilling* to work would be sent away without help.

Civil society may have a responsibility to provide employment opportunity for the undeserving poor. But by actually supporting those who prefer sloth to work, society will only increase the ranks of the undeserving poor.

Paul speaks of this distinction in a letter to the Thessalonians:

In the name of the Lord Jesus Christ, we command you, brothers and sisters, to keep away from every believer who is idle and disruptive and does not live according to the teaching you received from us. . . . For even when we were with you, we gave you this rule: "The one who is unwilling to work shall not eat." We hear that some among you are idle and disruptive. They are not busy; they are busybodies. Such people we command and urge in the Lord Jesus Christ to settle down and earn the food they eat. And as for you, brothers and sisters, never tire of doing what is good. (2 Thess. 3:6, 10–13)

Notice the balance. Never tire of doing what is right; always be involved. But distinguish between the laboring poor and the undeserving poor; this is compassion for both.

Having said that, we must take care not to push this concept too far. A spirit of grace must influence Christ followers as we engage with people. Timothy Keller points out that no one who has experienced God's grace—God's unmerited favor—should be quick to label another human being as unworthy of help.

DISCERNMENT

STUDY GUIDE
SESSION 13

The fourth principle, which arises from God's nature as trustworthy and true, is discernment. We read in Jeremiah 17:9, "The heart is deceitful above all things and beyond cure. Who can understand it?" The human heart is wicked. John wrote, "If we claim to be without sin, we deceive ourselves and the truth is not in us. . . . If we claim we have not sinned, we make [God] out to be a liar and his word is not in us" (1 John 1:8, 10). We humans deceive ourselves. We create worlds of illusion. We need discernment, which can be thought of as the means of categorization. We must be discerning, because many people manipulate the system. Welfare fraud and manipulation need to be recognized and exposed.

Years ago my wife, Marilyn, and I had a layover in Luxembourg on our way home from Europe. We were having dinner at a table with a man who was on his way to New York to collect his welfare payments. He had been on welfare for years. His checks simply piled up until he traveled back to the United States, picked them up, and returned to Europe to play.

Such misuse of money earned by the honest labor of others is encouraged by arm's-length government programs. Indiscriminate aid, no matter how well intentioned, too often fosters abuse and breeds dependence and poverty. Sentimentality leads to foolish compassion. As our friends at PovertyCure are fond of saying: "Good intentions do not end poverty!"[14] Discernment, on the other hand, prevents the kind of folly that rewards people who cheat the system. The issue of poverty must be tackled with the head as well as the heart. The heart can lead us to see the need and be moved with compassion. The head will help us discern the best way to approach the solving of the problem.

Before we start any charitable activity, we would do well to ask ourselves, *Who are we doing this for? Are we working to empower the poor or to relieve the guilt of the benefactor?* Too much charity is done so that donors can feel good about themselves and their generosity. But "charity" is another way to say "love," and love by definition is selfless. Love is about serving others, not making yourself feel good.

Walter Williams, professor of economics at George Mason University, put it this way: "To be compassionate to a person, in the long run, you have to be dispassionate in your analysis."[15] He gives a hypothetical example. Suppose a doctor had friends whose eleven-year-old daughter was an aspiring ballerina. If they brought her to him with cancer in her leg, and he said, "I will be compassionate. I will not cut off her leg so she can continue to dance," the girl would die. True compassion requires objective evaluation and decisions: "If you want your daughter to live, I have to do the surgery. She may not be able to dance, but she will live." Sometimes only dispassionate assessment allows for the most compassionate response. Williams continues, "We have to think with our brains instead of our hearts when we approach the problems of poverty."[16] Our hearts can stir us to the need, but if our hearts design the programs, we will probably disempower people. If we don't keep a balance between a tender heart and a clear head, we'll likely increase the poverty.

Another application of the principle of discernment comes from Luis Sena, a longtime friend and former Food for the Hungry country director in the Dominican Republic. As Luis once said, "It is important to discriminate between those communities which are seeking to develop themselves and those which are seeking handouts." What a difference we would see if this simple distinction were consistently applied.

Discernment and dispassionate analysis will also help us realize that not all who are physically poor are truly poor. Human development has its own math. Jesus said, "Blessed are you who are poor, for yours is the kingdom of God. Blessed are you who hunger now, for you will be satisfied. Blessed are you who weep now, for you will laugh" (Luke 6:20–21).

On one occasion during my work with Food for the Hungry, I took a group of Hunger Corps trainees to a village in Mexico that had no running water or electricity. On the first night we debriefed the day's activities while standing a few yards away from a house made of scrap building materials. While we were there, a dozen local people gathered outside the house and began singing hymns, accompanied by a sixteen-year-old boy playing a guitar. Our group joined them. A mother would call out a child's name and a scripture reference, and the child would stand and recite the verses. Then they would sing another hymn. This was repeated several times. Later, back at our tents, we sat down. For some time we conversed together around the question, "What did we see here?" We agreed that in our busy US lives this scene would never have happened. We have so many things to protect—our fancy houses and our fancy cars—that we can miss out on true wealth.

We need to be discerning. Richard Stearns writes: "Perhaps the greatest mistake commonly made by those who strive to help the poor is the failure to see the assets and strengths that are always present in people and their communities no matter how poor they are. Seeing their glass as half full rather than half empty can completely change our approach to helping."[17] People who are materially poor by our standards may in fact be much wealthier than we are.

EMPLOYMENT

The fifth principle is employment. God is a creative God, and we are made in his image. He made us to work. Work brings dignity to the individual and abundance to society.[18] In Genesis we find these words: "The LORD God took the man and put him in the Garden of Eden to work it and take care of it" (Gen. 2:15). When did God put man in the garden to take care of it? Before the fall, not after. Work has been important from the beginning of human creation. The preacher of Ecclesiastes says, "So I saw that there is nothing better for a person than to enjoy their work, because that is their lot. For who can bring them to see what will happen after them?" (Eccles. 3:22). In God's economy, human work is our sacred calling. Employment matters. Nothing creates dependency faster than to deny individuals their labor or the fruit of their labor.

from the recent experiences of socialist and 'third world' countries, in their theory that a free and prosperous economy does more to raise people above the poverty line than government decrees and regulations."[22] Governments and institutions that disempower the poor were never God's intention.

GOD

Compassion, the ground of true social justice, has an ancient derivation: it comes from God. As we saw earlier, God gives us this picture of his nature: "The LORD, the LORD, the compassionate and gracious God, slow to anger, abounding in love and faithfulness, maintaining love to thousands, and forgiving wickedness, rebellion and sin. Yet he does not leave the guilty unpunished; he punishes the children and their children for the sin of the parents to the third and the fourth generation" (Exod. 34:6–7).

Gary Haugen, president of International Justice Mission, highlights four truths about God's character which inform our view of social justice. First, "God loves justice and, conversely, hates injustice."[23] It is vital to recognize that God is not impassive; his zeal for justice springs from his very heart. Second, "God has compassion for those who suffer injustice—everywhere around the world, without distinction or favor."[24] Consider, for example, Psalm 67:4: "May the nations be glad and sing for joy, for you rule the peoples with equity and guide the nations of the earth." Third, "God judges and condemns those who perpetrate injustice."[25] The apostle Paul could confidently say, "Alexander the metalworker did me a great deal of harm. The Lord will repay him for what he has done" (2 Tim. 4:14). Finally, "God seeks active rescue for the victims of injustice."[26] We see this in God's declaration to Moses: "I have indeed seen the misery of my people in Egypt. I have heard them crying out because of their slave drivers, and I am concerned about their suffering. So I have come down to rescue them from the hand of the Egyptians" (Exod. 3:7–8).

All compassion springs from the heart of God. God's character, as we've seen in Exodus 34, includes compassion and its related virtue, love.

God has manifested his compassion in the incarnation. We saw that most clearly when Christ, the suffering Servant, came to suffer with us and for us. What is more, cultures and people become like the god they worship. A God-honoring culture is compassionate; a world without Christ is a world without compassion. We are called to be like our compassionate God. As one writer has put it, "Our happiness, God's glory, and loving our neighbors are all bound together."[27]

Timothy Keller points out that God identifies himself as compassionate and that the same standard is to apply to God's people.

> God often tells the Israelites to lend to the poor without interest and to distribute goods to the needy and to defend the fatherless, because "the LORD your God . . . defends the cause [*mishpat*] of the fatherless and the widow, and loves the foreigner, giving them food and clothing" (Deut. 10:17–18). If this is true of God, we who believe in him must always find some way of expressing it in our own practices, even if believers now live in a new stage in the history of God's redemption.[28]

Count Zinzendorf (whom we saw in chapter 3), reflecting on what Christ had borne for him, responded with a full-life obedience. What about you? Jesus Christ has died for you. He has suffered for you. He wants to suffer together with you. Now he asks, "What will you do for me?"

Gary Haugen points out that sometimes we miss this link between the injustice and suffering around us and our own responsibility to address it. With the psalmist we cry, "Why, LORD, do you stand far off? Why do you hide yourself in times of trouble?" (Ps. 10:1). Haugen says, "But gradually it has occurred to me that the problem may not be that God is far off; the problem may be that God's people are far off."[29]

The Bible does not lack pictures of Christian compassion. Isaiah 58 remains one of the most potent expressions of God's perspective on how his people should be responding toward the poor.

Is not this the kind of fasting I have chosen:
>   to loose the chains of injustice,
>   and untie the cords of the yoke,
> to set the oppressed free,
>   and break every yoke?
> Is it not to share your food with the hungry
>   and to provide the poor wanderer with shelter—
> when you see the naked, to clothe them,
>   and not to turn away from your own flesh and blood?
> (Isa. 58:6–7)

Consider also the well-known story of the good Samaritan from Luke 10, expounded earlier. The story could be summed up with the phrase *love is better than religion.* Timothy Keller asks, "What was Jesus doing with this story? He was giving a radical answer to the question, What does it mean to love your neighbor? What is the definition of 'love'? Jesus answered that by depicting a man meeting material, physical, and economic needs through deeds."[30]

Love shows itself with a generosity of spirit and a culture of compassion which is measured not by number of dollars but by nobility of character, quality of time, and value of service. The early church understood that compassion springs from the heart of God. Christians opened their homes and created hospices for people who were terminally ill. They visited people in prison, as the ministry Prison Fellowship does today. Church people moved into slums to live among the poor, as Food for the Hungry has done by sending Hunger Corps volunteers to live in poor communities in developing countries around the world.

Every Christian needs to respond as Zinzendorf did to Christ's question. Some will be led to begin a special ministry of hospitality, opening their homes to unwed mothers, orphans, or homeless people. Some will establish or serve in hospices for terminally ill people, including AIDS sufferers. Some will visit prisoners. Some will live in a slum or work among the poor in a developing country.

Something remarkable happened in the third century. Compassion did not exist as a concept in the Greco-Roman world until it was manifested by Christians. Emperor Julian recognized Christians as a whole new breed of people, referring to them as *atheists* because they refused to bow before the "god" Caesar. He wrote, "Atheism [i.e., Christianity] has been specially advanced through the loving service rendered to strangers, and through their care for the burial of the dead. It is a scandal that there is not a single Jew who is a beggar, and that the godless Galileans care not only for their own poor but for ours as well; while those who belong to us look in vain for the help that we should render them."[31] What an example!

The early church understood compassion because they knew the God of compassion. God's compassion made great demands on him. It took his Son to the cross. Christ's death provided for forgiveness, and those who were born again into his family became compassionate like him. Compassion sprang from their lives. They performed compassionate acts and created compassionate institutions, so much so that a godless emperor watching them reflected, *Here is a new kind of person, one we have never seen before.*

Richard Stearns of World Vision poses a series of questions that we must all seriously ask ourselves:

> How will the Church of Jesus Christ respond to the "lepers" in our midst—the poor, the sick, and the oppressed, in our country and in our world? Are we, like Christ, willing to respond with compassion and urgency to those who suffer? Are we willing? Do we have the kind of faith, the moral courage, the depth of love, and the strength of will to rise up off of our padded pews to demonstrate the good news to the world?[32]

If we do have that kind of faith, if we are willing to respond to injustice in our world, we must ask ourselves some further questions. What worldview do we hold, and how does it affect our understanding of social justice? Have we bought into a pessimistic, materialistic view of wealth and development? Do we see the government as the solution to our many problems? Or will we instead follow the examples of Christians throughout history and the example of Christ himself? Will we give our lives to the service of others, to see the will of God done on earth as it is in heaven?

May we grasp the biblical measure of compassion in our generation. May we be people who understand that compassion has sprung from the heart of God, that his compassion has been faithful throughout generations, that he has manifested it in the incarnation, and that now he wants to manifest it through our lives in a broken world.

CHAPTER 7

THE ACTION OF COMPASSION

We have examined the erosion of a biblical understanding and practice of social justice. As we near the end of this book, we want to
highlight some exceptions to this disturbing trend. Yes, Western societies
have lost much in terms of the practice of compassionate acts of Christ-
like love. Social justice is not what it once was.

STUDY GUIDE
SESSION 14

And yet God is still active in his world. As the old hymn goes,
"Though the wrong seems oft so strong, God is the ruler yet!" Here are
some vignettes of biblical compassion. We hope that these stories serve
two purposes: to model the principles we have discussed, and to give
hope. As you read, be encouraged to know that Christ followers in many
of the world's communities are resetting the understanding of compassion in some exciting ways.[1]

THE POWER OF LISTENING IN
A POOR RICH COUNTRY

Most people wouldn't list Japan as a poor country. Indeed, in 2013 the
Japanese income per capita was over US$46,000, compared to just $6,560
for China or $950 for Cambodia.[2]

But what if a nation's wealth were measured by more than money?
What if a nation's wealth were based on the strength of its citizens'

relationships? On the nation's character? The level of social peace? Justice for all? An increase in literacy and wisdom? In health? The hopefulness of its youth? The connection of its people to the living God? By such measures, Japan, and many other "rich" countries in our world, might be considered desperate.

Shun Jinnai helped found Friends with the Voiceless, the Japanese arm of the Disciple Nations Alliance.

Jinnai says Japan has the highest rate of suicide among the world's developed countries: more than 30,000 people kill themselves each year (the actual number is rumored to be double that, but family members often attribute such deaths to accidents or illness to avoid shame). About 85 percent of Japanese young people say they can't find meaning in their lives, and only 0.3 percent of the country's 120 million residents have a relationship with Christ.

"This is a result of the story that Japanese people have been following," says Jinnai. "The story is about economic sufficiency and individualism. That story turned out not to be trustworthy, all of a sudden," he says of March and April 2011, when the country suffered its most powerful recorded earthquake followed by a ferocious tsunami and the worst nuclear disaster since Chernobyl.

The cost was enormous: more than 18,000 human lives and about $235 billion.

"So, people of Japan are in a big question now," Jinnai says. "They are asking, how should we live now? Because we lost our story." He says what Japanese people need is "restoration of relationship . . . serving each other, like Jesus did, and the image of family that the Bible tells us."

Since 2004, Jinnai has employed local resources and bold creativity to reach lost and lonely Japanese people. That year, he heard a Disciple Nations Alliance (DNA) speaker and "was so touched by the concept that a church should care for the most broken in society," he says.

As a result, he went to a Tokyo train station and looked for broken people to help.

He gathered a few friends and looked for trash to pick up—anything to bring God's beauty, goodness, and truth to his community. After one month, the small group was ready to go deeper. They came back to the train station with a sign: "We will listen to you for free." They did this every Monday and Friday night after work for two years, sometimes lingering in conversations with strangers until 1:00 a.m.

They listened to people's struggles with anxiety or anger; often, teens would arrive wanting to discuss their parents' divorces or their broken families. Some visitors would ask why Jinnai and his friends were doing this, which opened the door for sharing their own stories of the freedom they had found in Christ.

Many of those visits led to people trusting Christ as their hope and salvation, then being baptized, and the ministry grew. As of March 2013, this ministry had dozens of volunteers working in twenty regions of Japan. Jinnai says they have seen more than one hundred Japanese come to the Lord each year through this simple outreach.

SOUTHEAST ASIAN CHURCH DOUBLES IN SIZE IN JUST ONE DAY[3]

In one area of southeast Asia, there was a small church made up of ten families. After they completed just the first DNA training, "Introduction to Wholistic Ministry," they wanted to show God's love to the family of a woman who was having heart surgery. The church decided to help in a very practical way: by harvesting the family's crops while the wife was recovering and the husband was tending to her in the hospital.

About thirty people from this tiny church worked in the couple's field—pulling up crops, bagging them, and delivering them to the couple's doorstep.

When the couple returned from the hospital, they were very surprised and moved, because they had worried about what to do with their crops. They had wondered how they would pay their large medical bills without the income of their harvest.

They said they wanted to believe in God because they had been seeking love but had never found any until they saw the love in the church.

The couple opened their hearts to Christ after receiving such a practical example of his sacrificial love for them. On top of that, nine other families in the community witnessed this event and also asked to receive Christ!

Praise the Lord who orchestrates all such events for his glory.

THE POWER OF A MUSTARD SEED

Rev. Meshack Okumu lives in Nairobi, Kenya, where he works for Carlile College's Centre for Urban Mission. He tells the following story. "We had a training in a slum called Mwiki Kasarani. About thirty-five pastors came. Most of the pastors are also working other jobs. One pastor was also a teacher in an informal school, so his immediate audience was the children in his school.

"The people coming from this community are so poor that sometimes the children would come to school without breakfast and sometimes would go without lunch. So this pastor and his members decided they would start making porridge for the children in this school. They said they would begin by making porridge for just ten children. The success of this porridge business was so good that the local government official (he is called the Chief) heard about it. The Chief then called the pastor/teacher and told him to come to his office for some relief food. They got about six bags of maize and six bags of beans. The pastor realized that you don't have to have everything, but when you begin being faithful with the very little that you have, God will multiply it.

"The pastor was excited that the Chief was able to hear and give them some food. They are continuing with the service of giving the children some light meals."

INTO THE RADIATION: LOVING, SACRIFICIAL SERVICE IN JAPAN

Dr. Eisuke Kanda is executive director of Friends with the Voiceless International (FVI), the national DNA-affiliated organization in Japan.

Following the March 2011 earthquake, tsunami, and radiation contamination, Dr. Kanda and his team went to Fukushima, the Japanese prefecture most threatened by nuclear radiation.

The city of Iwaki near the plant, population 350,000, saw more than 150,000 people flee because of the fear of radiation from the nuclear plant. Those who fled included many doctors and nurses as well as pastors. Of the thirty-five churches in the city, only four pastors remained. When asked why they remained, the following stories emerged.

Tiny Church Serves Large City

"Many people told Pastor S. to escape, but he dreamed that he saw Jesus walking toward the nuclear plant, bearing the cross. He woke up from this powerful dream and thought, *If Jesus is walking toward the nuclear plant, I should not escape; I should stay.* So he decided to stay.

"The next day he started getting lots of relief goods—water, food, etc.—from his denomination. His church building was soon filled with these goods. He didn't know what to do. So he put up a poster in front of his church, inviting anyone who wanted food, water, and other supplies to come and receive them without charge.

"People saw the poster, and he was amazed at the numbers who came. Few people knew anything about his little church, but some drove a half hour to his church for the food and water. At that time the city government was not operating or doing anything to help affected people. All the shops were closed. People had no way to get food.

"Pastor S. counted about 1,300 people who came to receive those relief goods. He says 'What I tried to do in ten years, God did in a few weeks.' In the first week, thirteen new people came to the Sunday service, an unheard-of result in a church of about twenty people. The next week, nine new people came. We met a few of those people. They said, 'Since coming to church, I feel peace here, I feel power here.'"

Loving Church Fills a Gap

"Pastor M. serves another church in Iwaki. A couple of years ago their building was destroyed when a neighboring house caught fire, so they had to move. They purchased a gambling hall with an empty first floor. They tried to borrow money to renovate the first floor, but the bank declined their request. Then March 11 came. They decided to use the whole first floor as a warehouse, and it was soon packed with relief goods from all over Japan, even from non-Christian sources.

"Because the city wasn't doing anything, this church became a center of food and water distribution. At that time, there were 4,000 refugees in 154 evacuation centers, and this church distributed 100,000 meals to these evacuees. Volunteers came not only from all over Japan but also from all over the world. The church housed them and sent them to the evacuation centers to serve the people. The weather was cold and no one had hot water for a bath, so the volunteers brought hot water to wash the feet of the people (as Jesus did for his disciples). They were able to have significant conversations with people as they washed their feet.

"As a result of their loving service, the church now has a very good relationship with the city government. In fact, the government is asking the church for advice about how to help the people."

SIMPLE ACTS OF LOVE IN THE NEIGHBORHOOD

A woman named Beatrice lives in a Nairobi slum called Kibera, reportedly one of the two largest slums in Africa. Beatrice took a DNA training course called "The Discipline of Love" and began thinking about how to implement the training in her community. But before she could share these ideas with her church, she felt she needed to begin doing something in her own surroundings.

Beatrice went to visit a neighbor and, to her surprise, found that the neighbor's children were sleeping on a carton on the floor without a mattress. She was moved, because in her home she had a mat, and she felt she needed to share it. She went home, took a knife, and cut in two the mat her children slept on. Through her sharing of what she had with her neighbor, a relationship developed. Neighbors who had once been distant were now talking to each other.

A pastor in the same training thought about the discipline of love. He had never visited his sick neighbor. This time he went back to his neighborhood and visited this neighbor. He found the neighbor was very sick and needed attention. But he didn't have money to take the neighbor to the hospital. So he went to another neighbor and asked if he could borrow 50 shillings (less than one dollar) for transport to the hospital. But that neighbor gave him 1000 shillings, which was enough to take a taxi instead of using public transport.

THE ACTION OF COMPASSION

These are just a few illustrations of how Christians are engaged in living and modeling compassion. In thousands of stories, Christians are showing compassion in the following ways:

- being first responders to natural and man-made disasters
- engaging in justice issues such as sex trafficking
- leading movements to end the horrors of gendercide and infanticide
- conserving and stewarding the earth
- fighting corruption and seeking to build consensus for the rule of law

How is social justice being reclaimed in your own community? What story will your own life contribute?

CHAPTER 8

POPE FRANCIS AND SOCIAL JUSTICE

In this final chapter, we want to highlight a current example of social justice—that of Pope Francis. The first Latin American to be elevated to the position of Bishop of Rome, he has been stirring a global discussion on social justice. On May 9, 2014, Pope Francis met in Rome with UN Secretary-General Ban Ki-moon and executives from the United Nations Agencies, Funds and Programmes. In his address,[1] the pope called upon the United Nations to contribute to a "worldwide ethical mobilization."

STUDY GUIDE SESSION 15

Much of the media focused on his call for the "legitimate redistribution of wealth" by the state. Sadly, many reports took this comment out of context. Francis is concerned about injustice. He called for "ethical mobilization," by which he means challenging all forms of injustice and resisting the "economy of exclusion," the "throwaway culture," and the "culture of death."

For the most part, Western media and academic institutions are informed by a naturalistic paradigm. All problems are reduced to material causes and solutions. There is little room for the ethical and moral standards of Judeo-Christian faith. Yet Pope Francis is calling out the common humanity of UN leaders, urging participation in a worldwide mobilization of morality.

Pope Francis began by saying:

Future Sustainable Development Goals must therefore be formulated and carried out with generosity and courage, so that they can have a real impact on the structural causes of poverty and hunger, attain more substantial results in protecting the environment, ensure dignified and productive labor for all, and provide appropriate protection for the family, which is an essential element in sustainable human and social development. Specifically, this involves challenging all forms of injustice and resisting the "economy of exclusion," the "throwaway culture" and the "culture of death" which nowadays sadly risk becoming passively accepted.

It is important to remember that evil is found in three forms. There is personal, moral evil, such as murder, theft, and adultery; institutional evil (what Pope Francis calls "structural causes") such as slavery, corruption, and sex trafficking; and natural evil, such as earthquakes, droughts, and tsunamis. All three forms of evil contribute to poverty and hunger. And all three forms of evil must be addressed. In his speech, the pope focused on institutional evil, within the larger context of the Judeo-Christian moral framework.

The pope identified the comprehensive and integrative nature of the problems faced by the human family. He recognized the need for environmental stewardship of the world and its resources. He acknowledged the dignity of work, the promotion of which entails fostering healthy work environments and nurturing a wide range of significant vocations. He also called for the protection of the family, which is under attack today on so many fronts.

Pope Francis continued by describing other forms of injustice found in the modern, materialistic culture. These include an "economy of exclusion," the "throwaway culture," and the "culture of death."

The "economy of exclusion" fails to recognize that humanity is founded on the Trinitarian principle of community: the One and Many God. Communities are comprised of individuals. The human family is a community of communities. Neither the distorted individualism of the modern West nor the collectivism of Marxist philosophy represents the ideal. Rather, we have a moral responsibility to care for people who are poor and to include them in the life of the community.

The "throwaway culture" is a reflection of the modern materialistic system of instant gratification and self-indulgence. Only material things have value. Man is basically a consuming animal. The hedonistic mantra—"let us eat, drink, and be merry for tomorrow we die"—is an apt description of life today. We work to consume. Many consumer goods are made of cheap plastic so they will need to be replaced quickly. Planned obsolescence is designed into our furniture, appliances, and automobiles. Quality goods built with excellence are rare; deferred gratification is rarer still. Our system supports an insatiable desire for more and more, now. Immediate gratification drives our modern consumer economies.

Our doctrine, derived from Darwin, is red in tooth and claw—the survival of the fittest. Pope Francis speaks of the "culture of death," an atheistic framework which yields no place for the right to life. According to this framework, we are here by some form of cosmic accident. The culture of death promotes human destruction in many forms: abortion, euthanasia, infanticide, and gendercide (200 million fewer females in the world are alive than should be). Life is the most fundamental right. Without an understanding of the dignity of all human life, from conception to natural death, there is no framework from which to fight the injustices of hunger and poverty. Without the right to life, there is no social justice.

All three of these injustices are derived from an atheistic, amoral culture. Without moral, thinking citizens, these injustices will become commonplace. They will weave even more tightly into the fabric of our existence. Thus the call by Pope Francis for an awakening of conscience:

> With this in mind, I would like to remind you, as representatives of the chief agencies of global cooperation, of an incident which took place two thousand years ago and is recounted in the Gospel of Saint Luke (19:1–10). It is the encounter between Jesus Christ and the rich tax collector Zacchaeus, as a result of

which Zacchaeus made a radical decision of sharing and justice, because his conscience had been awakened by the gaze of Jesus. This same spirit should be at the beginning and end of all political and economic activity.

Pope Francis retells the story of Jesus's confrontation with Zacchaeus, a Jew who collected taxes for the occupying Roman government. Zacchaeus was guilty on two counts. First, he was serving an oppressive foreign power, helping subjugate his own people. Second, he was corrupt. He collected more taxes than were due and pocketed the balance for himself.

As Pope Francis reminds us, "the gaze of Jesus" confronted Zacchaeus and prompted his repentance. While institutional evil needs to be addressed, the root of evil is found in man. It is the sin of individuals, running right through the heart and penetrating the mind of each person, that is the source of injustice in our societies.

We see this same confrontation and grace in Victor Hugo's novel *Les Misérables*. Bishop Myriel of Digne extends grace to the thief Jean Valjean. This marks the turning point in Jean Valjean's life, just as the confrontation with Jesus changed Zacchaeus. Valjean repents of his corruption and becomes a man of justice. It is this spirit of radical repentance that should frame our political and economic activity both personal and corporate. Individuals who takes responsibility for their own culpability can trigger a society's repenting of its collective, institutional evil.

Pope Francis continues his challenge:

Today, in concrete terms, an awareness of the dignity of each of our brothers and sisters whose life is sacred and inviolable from conception to natural death must lead us to share with complete freedom the goods which God's providence has placed in our hands, material goods but also intellectual and spiritual ones, and to give back generously and lavishly whatever we may have earlier unjustly refused to others.

Here Pope Francis roots social justice where it belongs. It does not derive from some arbitrary absolute of a tyrannical society but from the moral principle of the dignity of all human life. Dignity applies to all life, without exclusion for any reason, from conception to natural death. The sharing is not under compulsion but from "complete [human] freedom." The compulsion is intrinsically motivated, not extrinsically imposed. It is free human beings generously motivated by the grace of God, functioning from a culture of generosity, rather than greed, to love and serve their fellow human beings. Note that the "goods" we possess are the gifts of God's providence, and we are mere stewards of these goods for the benefit of creation and of our fellow human beings.

Note also that we are to share not simply material capital (as would be the case in a naturalistic framework). Pope Francis also mentions spiritual capital, which includes virtues, strength of character, gifts and fruit of the Spirit, the reality of the intervention of the living God in human affairs, and so on. He also speaks of intellectual capital: the human mind, including reason and analytical ability (the ability to "think God's thoughts after him"); belief systems, including worldview, thoughts, and ideas; wisdom (moral application of truth); and self-awareness. To these two types of capital, six more could be added:

- Natural capital: those resources in the ground, commonly called "natural resources," as well as the natural laws governing the created order that aid in our stewarding of creation.
- Moral capital (conscience): the ability to distinguish right from wrong, honesty and integrity, courage, fortitude, and so on.
- Economic capital: the human ability to create wealth, currencies, banks, securities markets, property (property rights, land title, copyright, etc.).
- Social capital: family and friends, communities, voluntary organizations (mosques, churches, synagogues, advocacy groups, service clubs, sports clubs), and community services (schools, libraries, museums, galleries, health clinics).

- Aesthetic capital: the ability to create and appreciate art, music, poetry, and literature; the ability to create secondary worlds like Tolkien's middle earth; the ability to appreciate beauty and the created universe.
- Institutional capital: government, civil laws, and infrastructure (roads, power grids, internet, etc.).

All these gifts of God are to be shared, not grudgingly as a selfish individual operating from a culture of greed would do, but lavishly, from a culture of generosity. God is a generous God. He lavishes grace upon us. He paid with the life of his Son Jesus to lavish grace upon us. Our thankful response is to be lavish in our generosity. As Jesus taught in Matthew 7:12, "So in everything, do to others what you would have them do to you, for this sums up the Law and the Prophets."

Now for the line of the pope's address that the media has focused on:

A contribution to this equitable development will also be made both by international activity aimed at the integral human development of all the world's peoples and by *the legitimate redistribution of economic benefits by the State* [emphasis mine], as well as indispensable cooperation between the private sector and civil society.

The world's elites focused here, especially on the phrase "the legitimate redistribution of economic benefits by the State." Pope Francis qualifies this call with his additional statement of the need for cooperation between the private sector and civil society.

As we have argued, an important distinction exists between the equity of all citizens before the law and equality of economic outcomes. The first promotes freedom; the second imposes state tyranny in an effort to force an artificial economic equality.

But what is the appropriate role of the state in determining economic outcomes? In the beginning at creation, human beings were made free and responsible. Today, too often the state, with good intentions of helping people who are poor, designs bureaucratic solutions that create dependencies, robbing people of their freedom and dignity. An illustration of this is the US War on Poverty.

In 1964, President Lyndon B. Johnson instituted a series of new government programs expanding on President Roosevelt's New Deal and offering more welfare assistance to the poor. In 1996, the Personal Responsibility and Work Opportunity Reconciliation Act initiated by the Republican congress and signed by President Bill Clinton added a work component to federal welfare programs. Despite the shift in requiring recipients to work, the mentality of solving poverty with money and large government programs endures.

As our country celebrated the fiftieth anniversary of Johnson's Great Society legislation, the outcome of the war on poverty was a tragic reminder that good intentions and the expenditure of money is not enough to "end poverty." In the executive summary of his 2012 paper "The American Welfare State: How We Spend Nearly $1 Trillion a Year Fighting Poverty—and Fail," researcher and author Michael Tanner of the Cato Institute states:

> News that the poverty rate has risen to 15.1 percent of Americans, the highest level in nearly a decade, has set off a predictable round of calls for increased government spending on social welfare programs. Yet this year the federal government will spend more than $668 billion on at least 126 different programs to fight poverty. And that does not even begin to count welfare spending by state and local governments, which adds $284 billion to that figure. In total, the United States spends nearly $1 trillion every year to fight poverty. That amounts to $20,610 for every poor person in America, or $61,830 per poor family of three.
>
> . . . Despite this government largess, more than 46 million Americans continue to live in poverty. Despite nearly $15 trillion [that's $15,000,000,000,000] in total welfare spending since Lyndon Johnson declared war on poverty in 1964, the poverty rate is perilously close to where we began more than 40 years ago.

Clearly we are doing something wrong. Throwing money at the problem has neither reduced poverty nor made the poor self-sufficient. It is time to reevaluate our approach to fighting poverty. We should focus less on making poverty more comfortable and more on creating the prosperity that will get people out of poverty.[2]

Help for people who are poor best comes from individuals, churches, synagogues, and other voluntary associations and company founders. Both the companies individuals establish and the voluntary associations they form are legitimate means of help for people in poverty. Their effectiveness was illustrated above by the social responsibility of the Arthur Guinness family and the brewery they founded.

In his speech, Pope Francis concluded:

Consequently, while encouraging you in your continuing efforts to coordinate the activity of the international agencies, which represents a service to all humanity, I urge you to work together in promoting a true, worldwide ethical mobilization which, beyond all differences of religious or political convictions, will spread and put into practice a shared ideal of fraternity and solidarity, especially with regard to the poorest and those most excluded.

Pope Francis ended his message by calling for a "worldwide ethical mobilization." He indicates that at their root, economic issues are moral issues. To see people and nations flourish requires a moral and ethical framework and commitment. The pope's call for fraternity and solidarity with the poorest of the poor is recognition of the one-and-many nature of the human community. He understands that the root of the word *compassion* is to suffer together with another person. These are helpful and biblical observations.

And yet in April 2014 the pope tweeted, "Inequality is the root of social evil."[3] But Judeo-Christian theism roots poverty in sin—the moral deficiency of the fallen human heart. Poverty is a result of violating God's created order. Social evil doesn't arise from inequality. Moral evil, not economic inequality, is the root of poverty. Commenting on the pope's tweet, Jewish theologian, writer, lecturer, and radio host Dennis Prager wrote, "The pope's tweet is from Marx, not Moses."[4]

So which is it?

This is something Pope Francis will need to clarify. Most of what he has argued in this piece is from the foundation of biblical principles. However, if he is saying that the state has a responsibility to forcibly redistribute economic benefits so that all people have the same outcome (a la Marx), that is a violation of the eighth and tenth commandments (a la Moses). This would indicate that his fallback economic framework is that of a closed universe.

In one sense, the current discussion in the church is between Marx and Moses. In light of the church's current debates on social justice, the goal of this book has been to bring our understanding and practice of social justice back into alignment with the Judeo-Christian worldview and the biblical concept of compassion, as expounded in Scripture and as practiced by the "great cloud of witnesses" throughout history. We have seen that social justice is about equity and not equality. It is about being equal before the law so that individuals may flourish according to their God-given gifts and callings. It is not about treating everyone the same, and thus forcing equal outcomes and uniformity in life. It is about creating conditions for human flourishing rather than building personal and institutional dependencies. It is about more than good intentions. It is about solutions that emancipate people from both mental and circumstantial poverty. It is about fostering the greatest gift of human potential and developing a mentality to create and responsibly share wealth.

In our generation, may we recommit our lives to both right biblical thinking and right biblical living. Let's reclaim social justice.

APPENDIX A: BIBLICAL WORDS
TRANSLATED "COMPASSION"

When studying the Scriptures, it is always wise to follow the historic pattern of inquiry by asking and answering three basic hermeneutical questions:

- What does the text say?
- What does the text mean?
- How does the text apply in my life and in the world?

The first question deals with biblical *exegesis*: bringing out of the text "the meaning the writers intended to convey and which their readers were expected to gather from it."[1] The second question has to do with *interpretation*. The third question deals with biblical *application*: showing how the text is to speak to people today in their own cultural setting.

Understanding what a text means entails knowing the definition and usage of key words. Since this book is about the biblical concept of compassion, it is good to take a few moments to review the Hebrew and Greek words translated "compassion." As in any language, there may be more than one meaning for a single word; that is the case for the Hebrew and Greek words translated "compassion."

Our English word *compassion* translates three words (or word families) from the Hebrew and four from the Greek. The following diagram captures the nexus (connected series) of biblical terms translated "compassion." The left side presents words from the New Testament; Old Testament words appear on the right. The four-digit numbers indicate codes from *Strong's Concordance*. Two of the three Old Testament word families have New Testament equivalents. These are indicated by the globes that straddle the line between the New and Old Testaments. The shaded globes refer to God's *loving-kindness,* the clear globes to God's *mercy.*

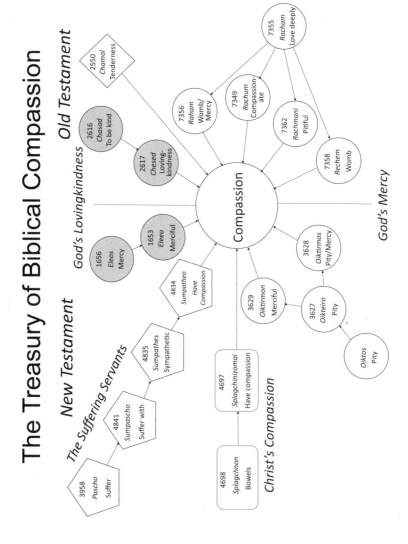

The Treasury of Biblical Compassion

We'll come to those equivalents, but let's begin with the diamond shape in the upper right corner. *Chamal* is an emotional response that results in action. Pharaoh's daughter, looking at the baby Moses (Exod. 2:6), demonstrated the meaning of *chamal*: "show mercy on, spare, take pity on, i.e., show kindness to one in an unfavorable, difficult, or dangerous situation, and so help or deliver in some manner; to treat with tenderness; to have compassion."[2]

Moving clockwise to the clear globes, we see that our word "mercy" comes from the Hebrew *racham*, "to love deeply." God is merciful because of his love. *Racham* means to have a feeling or attitude of strong affection based on an association or relationship. But the word indicates more than feeling or attitude. It manifests in action. It becomes an act of kindness toward the object of one's love and affection. *Racham* is used forty-four times in the Old Testament. For example, "Praise the LORD, my soul, and forget not all his benefits—who forgives all your sins, and heals all your diseases, who redeems your life from the pit, and crowns you with love and *compassion*" (Ps. 103:2–4, italics added).

Racham is translated "mercy, compassion, womb"! From the same root is derived *rechem*. Like *racham*, it can also be translated "womb, uterus." A third term from the same family is *rachum*, an adjective meaning "compassionate, merciful, and favorable." In other words, one who is *rachum* shows favor in place of deserved punishment. This word, appearing thirteen times in the Old Testament, is *only used of God*. The final member of the *racham* family, found only once, is *rachamani*, "full of pity."

Next we move clockwise into the Greek terms equivalent to the Hebrew *racham*. The verb *oiktiro* comes from *oiktos* (pity). *Oiktiro* has two spin-off terms. The Greek noun *oiktirmos*[3] means "mercy" as in the mercy of God. The adjective, *oiktirmon*, occurs three times and is translated "merciful" and "of tender mercy." James 5:11 provides an example: "As you know, we count as blessed those who have persevered. You have heard of Job's perseverance and have seen what the Lord finally brought about. The Lord is full of compassion and *mercy*" (italics added).

The next family includes two words pictured in the rectangles. One term is *splagchnizomai*, a verb meaning to "feel compassion for, have pity on, have one's heart go out to." This word is used twelve times. It is derived from *splagchnon*, "desires, compassion, tender mercies, affection."[4]

The pentagonal shapes depict another word family, this one rooted in the term *pascho*,[5] a verb meaning "to suffer, to undergo an experience implying suffering," which is used forty-two times. Included in this family are the adjective, *sumpathes* (sympathetic) and two verbs. The first, *sumpatheo*, means "to have a fellow feeling with," that is, "sympathize with." The second verb, *sumpascho*, means "to suffer with."

Finally, at the top of the diagram in the shaded globes are another pair of relevant word families mirrored in each testament, words that speak of God's loving-kindness: the Hebrew *chasad* and the Greek *eleos*.

Chasad occurs three times in the Old Testament. The King James translates it "show thyself merciful" twice and "put to shame" once. It means "to be good, to be kind." The main derivative of *chasad* is the better-known noun *chesed*. This term, which occurs 248 times in the Old Testament, is difficult to translate into English. It means "loyal love, unfailing kindness, devotion." The KJV translates it as "mercy" 149 times, "kindness" forty times, "loving-kindness" thirty times, and "goodness" twelve times. *Chesed* is used of God and his actions toward humans. It is the outgoing kindness of the heart of God. In Psalm 136 this word appears twenty-six times, once in each verse (and twenty-five of those times, *chesed* is accompanied by *emeth*, "truth," that is, not merely intellectual truth, but truth in the sense of fidelity or steadfastness).

The Greek equivalent of *chesed* is the verb *eleeo*. Found thirty-one times in the New Testament, *eleeo*[6] means "to show mercy to, to show pity." *Eleeo* is derived from *eleos*. It occurs twenty-eight times and means "mercy, kindness, or good will toward the miserable and the afflicted." It carries the idea of wanting to help those in need. This word is often applied to mercy between humans: "Blessed are the merciful, for they will be shown mercy" (Matt. 5:7).

APPENDIX B: IDEA SHIFTS AND ACCOMPANYING LANGUAGE SHIFTS

IDEA SHIFT	LANGUAGE SHIFT
Love of God → Love of humanity	Moral/religious → Secular
	Compassion → Sentiment
Personal → Impersonal	Poor person (individual) → The poor (a class)
	Unemployed (person) → Unemployment (a condition)
Moral → Structural	Individual responsibility → Class responsibility
Moral philosophy → Political economy	Private solutions → Public solutions
	Empowerment → Entitlement
Equality before God/law → Equality of outcomes	Justice → (welfare) Rights
	Equity → (numerical) Equality
Sharing time & self → Sharing money	Relationships → Dollars

APPENDIX C: COMMENTS AND RESPONSES FROM THE *DARROW MILLER AND FRIENDS* BLOG

We include here some relevant discussion that originally appeared on the *Darrow Miller and Friends* blog (darrowmillerandfriends.com).

COMMENT: Can we put all underpinning beliefs related to social justice into a 2 x 2 box? Yes, God (sometimes) works through a supernatural "open" process and through "moral" people, but surely we have sometimes seen the poor cared for by "amoral" atheists.

RESPONSE: This is true. People who are immoral sometimes act morally and people who profess to act by a moral standard at times do not. But in each case the person is acting apart from the implication of their framework. What do I mean? An atheistic-materialistic framework provides no basis to do good or to pursue justice. That framework, by its nature, encourages "the survival of the fittest" and sees nature as "red in tooth and claw." The propensity is toward the accumulation and use of power; the goal is to survive, to come out on top. Atheists who function compassionately are doing so from their human nature as given by God and not as an impulse from their atheistic framework.

COMMENT: There are millions of well-meaning Christians who pity the poor as simply lacking material resources, and who think the solution is to go on a mission trip to build stuff for them.

RESPONSE: Yes. Often these folks are motivated by Christ, but they do not reflect on what they are doing, and thus they tend to create more poverty. Steve Corbett and Brian Fikkert of the Chalmers Center have written a book, *When Helping Hurts*, which responds to these well-intentioned mistakes.

COMMENT: Isn't it oversimplification to split people into Judeo-Christian or atheistic-materialistic paradigms? Doesn't that miss the possibility that people (and belief systems) are more complex and nuanced? For example, solving material poverty will certainly require creation of wealth through development of human skills, but may also require that government play a proper role in protecting society's most vulnerable citizens.

RESPONSE: Systems of truth claims are very complex. In some ways this is good. At the same time it provides challenges. Yes, these systems may be nuanced, but the nature of the nuances will conform to the boundaries which define each system.

It is important for government to protect via the rule of law. Each person, rich or poor, healthy or sickly, young or old, female or male, black or white, is to be equal before the law. It is the government's priority to provide justice and social peace so that free citizens can pursue the health and prosperity of their families in a framework of economic freedom.

Here's a perspective on levels of responsibility that a society would do well to observe. First, we must practice personal responsibility at an individual level. After that comes family responsibility, followed by the responsibility of voluntary associations such as churches, synagogues, mosques, boys and girls clubs, and civic clubs. Only then should government responsibility be invoked in providing a safety net, and even then the responsibility of local government should precede that of state government. Federal government begins only after that. Part of the beauty of this model is that those who are closer to the need can provide more personal help. Unfortunately today, in the United States and other places, we assume the federal government is the party responsible to solve problems. So the solutions tend to be bureaucratic and top-down. Money replaces personal responsibility.

Here's a question that frames part of the battle we are facing in the United States today: Will our citizens be responsible? Will they be free and "large" human beings, or will the government continue to take on more and more responsibility that belongs elsewhere? In such a scenario the government grows and people shrink to insignificance.

NOTES

FOREWORD

1. G. K. Chesterton, *The Ball and the Cross* (Eastford, CT: Martino Fine Books, 2011), 96.
2. Abraham Kuyper, "Sphere Sovereignty," in James D. Bratt, *Abraham Kuyper: A Centennial Reader* (Grand Rapids: Eerdmans, 1988), 488.
3. Dietrich Bonhoeffer, *Ethics* (New York: Touchstone, 1995), 19.

PREFACE

1. darrowmillerandfriends.com

INTRODUCTION

1. Ken Wytsma, *Pursuing Justice: The Call to Live and Die for Bigger Things* (Nashville: Thomas Nelson, 2013), 212.

CHAPTER I: WHAT IS SOCIAL JUSTICE?

1. C. S. Lewis, *Of Other Worlds: Essays and Stories*, ed. Walter Hooper (New York: Harcourt, 1975), 38. Lewis appears to have been writing about Chinese Communists' persecution of Western Christian missionaries who preached the gospel but did not help the poor.
2. Timothy Keller, *Generous Justice: How God's Grace Makes Us Just* (New York: Riverhead Books, 2010), xi.
3. Michael Novak, "Social Justice: Not What You Think It Is," Heritage Lectures, The Heritage Foundation, December 29, 2009, http://www.heritage.org/research/lecture/social-justice-not-what-you-think-it-is.
4. Ken Wytsma, *Pursuing Justice: The Call to Live and Die for Bigger Things* (Nashville: Thomas Nelson, 2013), 9.
5. Udo Middelmann, in a spring 2012 letter to friends of the Francis A. Schaeffer Foundation.
6. Thomas Aquinas, *Summa Theologica* (New York: Cosimo Classics, 2007), 1432.
7. Ryan Messmore, "Real Social Justice," On the Square, *First Things*, November 26, 2010, http://www.firstthings.com/onthesquare/2010/11/real-social-justice.
8. Michael Novak describes this unfolding in his essay "Social Justice: Not What You Think It Is."

9. "Global Redistribution as a Solution to Poverty," *IDS in Focus Policy Briefing* 11 (October 2009): 1, http://www.ids.ac.uk/files/dmfile/IF11.1web.pdf.

10. C. S. Lewis, *The Screwtape Letters*, illustrated ed. (London: HarperCollins, 2009), 221.

CHAPTER 2: PARADIGMS OF SOCIAL JUSTICE

1. For example, systems such as standardized application forms, project proposals, and logistics infrastructure, which make it easy for recipients to receive aid.

2. The German philosopher Friedrich Nietzsche (1844–1900) believed that the primary driving force in humans was the universal "will to power," i.e., ambition, the desire to conquer and come out on top.

3. Richard Dawkins, *The Selfish Gene* (Oxford: University Press, 2006), 2.

4. Michael Novak, "Don't Confuse the Common Good with Statism," *Juicy Ecumenism: The Institute on Religion and Democracy's Blog*, October 3, 2011, http://www.juicyecumenism.com/2011/10/03/dont-confuse-the-common-good-with-statism/.

5. "SPIEGEL Interview with African Economics Expert: 'For God's Sake, Please Stop the Aid!,'" Spiegel Online, July 4, 2005, http://www.spiegel.de/international/spiegel/spiegel-interview-with-african-economics-expert-for-god-s-sake-please-stop-the-aid-a-363663.html.

6. Steve Chapman, "Toward the Conquest of World Poverty," *Reason*, March 29, 2012, http://reason.com/archives/2012/03/29/toward-the-conquest-of-world-poverty.

7. PovertyCure, *From Aid to Enterprise*, http://youtu.be/UxASM44gPlU.

8. "Mission of PovertyCure," PovertyCure, http://www.povertycure.org/about/.

9. Vishal Mangalwadi, *Truth and Transformation: A Manifesto for Ailing Nations* (Seattle: YWAM Publishing, 2009), 41.

10. "The classic understanding [of revival] is that of a period of unusual and heightened spiritual activity in a section of the church, brought about by a renewing and empowering work of the Holy Spirit, bringing a new sense of the presence of God, especially in his holiness, resulting in a deeper awareness of sin in the lives of believers, followed by new joy as sin is confessed and forgiven." *Evangelical Dictionary of Theology*, 2nd ed. (Grand Rapids: Baker, 2001), 1025.

11. "The act of reforming; correction or amendment of life, manners, or of any thing vicious or corrupt; as the reformation of manners." *Webster's*.

12. Stephen Mansfield, *The Search for God and Guinness: A Biography of the Beer that Changed the World* (Nashville: Thomas Nelson, 2009).

13. Oswald Chambers, *My Utmost for His Highest* (Grand Rapids: Discovery House, 1992), June 27 entry.

CHAPTER 3: THE DEMISE OF SOCIAL JUSTICE

1. Quoted by Marvin Olasky, *The Tragedy of American Compassion* (Washington: Regnery Gateway, 1992), 225.
2. Thomas Sowell, "Cold Compassion," *Forbes*, August 2, 1993, 67.
3. Quoted by Gertrude Himmelfarb, *Poverty and Compassion: The Moral Imagination of the Late Victorians* (New York: Alfred A. Knopf, 1991), 3.
4. Gary A. Haugen, *Good News about Injustice: A Witness of Courage in a Hurting World* (Downers Grove, IL: InterVarsity Press, 1999), 143.
5. Noah Webster was considered the father of American education, one of the founding fathers of the United States, and the lexicographer of a new nation. His dictionary, first published in 1828, was decades in the making and was titled *An American Dictionary of the English Language*.
6. Merriam-Webster, www.merriam-webster.com/dictionary/compassion.
7. Cambridge Dictionaries Online, dictionary.cambridge.org/us/dictionary/american-english/compassion.
8. Oxford Dictionaries, www.oxforddictionaries.com/us/definition/american_english/compassion.
9. "Why Practice Compassion?" Greater Good Science Center (University of California, Berkley), http://greatergood.berkeley.edu/topic/compassion/definition#why_practice.
10. See Darrow Miller, *Discipling Nations: The Power of Truth to Transform Cultures* (Seattle: YWAM Publishing, 2001), 45–47.
11. Olasky, *Tragedy of American Compassion*, 54–55.
12. Ibid.
13. Ken Wytsma, *Pursuing Justice: The Call to Live and Die for Bigger Things* (Nashville: Thomas Nelson, 2013), 47.
14. Leo Tolstoy, *The Meaning of the Russian Revolution*, chapter 12, http://www.nonresistance.org/docs_htm/Tolstoy/~Meaning_of_Russian_Revolution/MRR_chapter12.html.
15. C. S. Lewis, *The Weight of Glory* (New York: Macmillan, 1980), 19.

CHAPTER 4: HOW A CORRUPTED WORSHIP ADULTERATED OUR COMPASSION

1. Marvin Olasky, *The Tragedy of American Compassion* (Washington: Regnery Gateway, 1992), 8.
2. Ibid., 8–9.
3. Ken Wytsma, *Pursuing Justice: The Call to Live and Die for Bigger Things* (Nashville: Thomas Nelson, 2013), 94–95.
4. Quoted by Gertrude Himmelfarb, *Poverty and Compassion: The Moral Imagination of the Late Victorians* (New York: Alfred A. Knopf, 1991), 182.
5. Ibid., 240.
6. Olasky, *Tragedy of American Compassion*, 121.

7.   Ibid., 67.

8.   Ibid., 68.

9.   Ibid.

10. For example, see her book, *The Pivot of Civilization*, which includes the following on pages 116–17. "[Charity] encourages the healthier and more normal sections of the world to shoulder the burden of unthinking and indiscriminate fecundity of others; which brings with it, as I think the reader must agree, a dead weight of human waste. Instead of decreasing and aiming to eliminate the stocks that are most detrimental to the future of the race and the world, it tends to render them to a menacing degree dominant." *The Pivot of Civilization* (New York: Brentano's, 1922). Or see George Grant, *Grand Illusions: The Legacy of Planned Parenthood* (Brentwood, TN: Wolgemuth & Hyatt, 1988).

11. Himmelfarb, *Poverty and Compassion*, 41–42.

12. Ibid., 4.

13. For more on this, see Scott Wisley, "Aid That Increases Poverty? A Case Study in Unintended Consequences," *Darrow Miller and Friends*, May 21, 2012, http://darrowmillerandfriends.com/2012/05/21/why-poverty-because-lies/.

14. See the Four P diagram on page 32.

15. Himmelfarb, *Poverty and Compassion*, 42.

16. Ibid., 102.

17. Olasky, *Tragedy of American Compassion*, 221.

18. Ibid., 147.

19. Alexis de Tocqueville, *Democracy in America* (London: Penguin Books, 2003), 593–95.

20. Ibid., 596.

21. "The professional social workers' contribution to the destruction of voluntarism is an acknowledged but embarrassing fact in some books that recount social work history." Olasky, *Tragedy of American Compassion*, 268.

22. Himmelfarb, *Poverty and Compassion*.

23. Olasky observes: "As professionals began to dominate the realm of compassion, volunteers began to depart. . . . Agencies began to report a dearth of volunteers, while at the same time narrowing the field for those who did volunteer. At the United Charities of Chicago by 1915, 'interested laymen were as likely to be consigned to a desk job as they were to be assigned to a family.' When board members at one charity organization wanted more involvement, its president announced, 'Our staff is so well organized that there is very little for our Board Members to do. . . .' Boards did retain one major function: 'Under the exacting gaze of a freshly certified professional elite, boards were remodeled into fund-raising bodies.'" Olasky, *Tragedy of American Compassion*, 146–47.

24. Daniel J. Smith and Daniel Sutter, "Response and Recovery after the Joplin Tornado: Lessons Applied and Lessons Learned," *Independent Review* 18, no. 2 (Fall 2013), http://www.independent.org/pdf/tir/tir_18_02_01_smith.pdf.

25. Ibid.

26. Gary A. Haugen, *Good News about Injustice: A Witness of Courage in a Hurting World* (Downers Grove, IL: InterVarsity Press, 1999), 63.

27. For more on this, see Darrow L. Miller, *Emancipating the World: A Christian Response to Radical Islam and Fundamentalist Atheism* (Seattle: YWAM Publishing, 2012), 75.

28. Thomas Malthus, *An Essay on the Principle of Population* (1798), www.marxists.org/reference/subject/economics/malthus/ch01.htm.

29. Himmelfarb, *Poverty and Compassion*, 300–301.

30. Ibid., 301.

CHAPTER 5: RADICAL SOCIAL JUSTICE: THE BIBLICAL IMPERATIVE

1. For further insights, including the more technical vocabulary details, see appendix A.

2. For more on this subject, see Darrow Miller's *Nurturing the Nations: Reclaiming the Dignity of Women in Building Healthy Cultures* (Downers Grove, IL: IVP Books, 2008).

3. J. Swanson, *Dictionary of Biblical Languages with Semantic Domains: Hebrew (Old Testament)*, electronic ed. (Oak Harbor, WA: Logos Research Systems, 1997).

4. James Tillman, "New Report Suggests Over 1 Billion Abortions Committed: Pro-Life Activists," LifeSiteNews.com, October 16, 2009, https://www.lifesitenews.com/news/new-report-suggests-over-1-billion-abortions-committed-pro-life-activists.

5. William Barclay, *The Beatitudes and the Lord's Prayer for Everyman* (New York: Harper & Row, 1963), 61

6. Ibid., 63.

7. Colin Brown, ed., *Dictionary of New Testament Theology* (Grand Rapids: Zondervan, 1971), 3:724 (italics added).

8. Barclay, *Beatitudes*, 67–68.

9. Ibid., 68.

10. Ibid.

11. Ibid., 69.

12. Ibid.

13. Ibid., 69–70.

14. Ibid., 70.

15. Ibid., 67.

16. Walter Brueggemann, *The Prophetic Imagination* (Philadelphia: Fortress, 1978), 85 (italics original).

CHAPTER 6: PRINCIPLES OF COMPASSION

1. For more on this topic, see Darrow Miller, *Discipling Nations: The Power of Truth to Transform Cultures* (Seattle: YWAM Publishing, 2001).

2. Timothy Keller, *Generous Justice: How God's Grace Makes Us Just* (New York: Riverhead Books, 2010), 19.

3. Gertrude Himmelfarb, *Poverty and Compassion: The Moral Imagination of the Late Victorians* (New York: Alfred A. Knopf, 1991), 18.

4. Marvin Olasky, *The Tragedy of American Compassion* (Washington: Regnery Gateway, 1992), 220.

5. Personal conversation with author.

6. "Our Vision," Redeemer Presbyterian Church, http://www.redeemer.com/learn/about_us/vision_and_values#vision.

7. Olasky, *Tragedy of American Compassion*, 102.

8. Ibid., 115.

9. Keller, *Generous Justice*, 109.

10. *Louw-Nida Greek-English Lexicon of the New Testament Based on Semantic Domains*, 2nd ed., ed. J. P. Louw and E. A. Nida (New York: United Bible Societies, 1988).

11. Keller, *Generous Justice*, 4.

12. Richard Stearns, *The Hole in Our Gospel* (Nashville: Thomas Nelson, 2009), 107.

13. As Timothy Keller points out, the Old Testament description of gleaning is another way to frame this approach: "Gleaning . . . enabled the poor to provide for themselves without relying on benevolence. On the other hand, Deuteronomy 23:24–25 protected the landowner from those who might try to over-glean. The Bible is not a classist tract that sees the rich as always the villains and the poor as always virtuous." Keller, *Generous Justice*, 111.

14. PovertyCure, *From Aid to Enterprise*, http://youtu.be/UxASM44gPlU.

15. From an interview with E. Calvin Beisner in *Christian Perspectives*, Liberty University, Winter 1990, 6.

16. Ibid.

17. Stearns, *Hole in Our Gospel*, 128.

18. See the video *Freedom to Flourish* by the Institute for Faith, Work & Economics, http://tifwe.org/news/inspirational-new-video-freedom-to-flourish/.

19. Olasky, *Tragedy of American Compassion*, 229. See also "Washington Journal; Shoeshine Businessman Standing Tall in Victory," *New York Times*, April 19, 1989, www.nytimes.com/1989/04/19/us/washington-journal-shoeshine-businessman-standing-tall-in-victory.html; Clint Block,

"A Triumph for Bootstraps Capitalism," *The Freeman*, October 1, 1989, http://fee.org/the_freeman/detail/a-triumph-for-bootstraps-capitalism/; Ego Shine, www.egoshoeshine.com.

20. For more on this concept, see Scott Allen and Darrow Miller, *The Forest in the Seed: A Biblical Perspective on Resources and Development* (Phoenix: Disciple Nations Alliance, 2006), available for free at http://www.disciple nations.org/resources/free-downloadable-books-bible-studies/.

21. Eugene H. Methvin, "Crusader for Peru's Have-Nots," *Reader's Digest*, January 1989, 139.

22. Himmelfarb, *Poverty and Compassion*, 389.

23. Haugen, *Good News about Injustice*, 69.

24. Ibid.

25. Ibid., 70.

26. Ibid.

27. Ken Wytsma, *Pursuing Justice: The Call to Live and Die for Bigger Things* (Nashville: Thomas Nelson, 2013), 55.

28. Keller, *Generous Justice*, 22.

29. Haugen, *Good News about Injustice*, 100.

30. Keller, *Generous Justice*, 67.

31. Stephen Neill, *A History of Christian Missions* (London: Penguin Books, 1966), 42.

32. Stearns, *Hole in Our Gospel*, 240.

CHAPTER 7: THE ACTION OF COMPASSION

1. These stories first appeared at Disciple Nations Alliance, www.disciple nations.org.

2. "Countries and Economies," The World Bank, http://data.worldbank.org/country.

3. This story comes from Disciple Nations Alliance partners in Southeast Asia, Reconciled World, through whom more than one thousand local churches are being discipled. God is vibrantly on the move. For the safety of our partners and local believers, we are not disclosing the specific country.

CHAPTER 8: POPE FRANCIS AND SOCIAL JUSTICE

1. "Pope Francis to United Nations Officials: Full Text," CatholicVote, www.catholicvote.org/pope-francis-to-un-officials-full-text/.

2. Michael Tanner, "The American Welfare State: How We Spend Nearly $1 Trillion a Year Fighting Poverty—and Fail," *Policy Analysis* 694 (April 11, 2012): 1, www.cato.org/sites/cato.org/files/pubs/pdf/PA694.pdf.

3. Pope Francis's Twitter page, April 28, 2014, https://twitter.com/pontifex/status/460697074585980928.

4. Dennis Prager, "Pope Francis, the Climate, and Leftism," *National Review Online*, January 6, 2015, http://www.nationalreview.com/article/395779/pope-francis-climate-and-leftism-dennis-prager.

APPENDIX A: BIBLICAL WORDS TRANSLATED "COMPASSION"

1. Walter A. Elwell, ed., *Evangelical Dictionary of Theology* (Grand Rapids: Baker Academic, 2001), 611, s.v. "exegesis."
2. Unless otherwise noted, biblical language definitions in this section are from J. Swanson, *Dictionary of Biblical Languages with Semantic Domains: Hebrew (Old Testament)*, electronic ed. (Oak Harbor, WA: Logos Research Systems, 1997).
3. Colin Brown, ed., *The New International Dictionary of New Testament Theology* (Zondervan: Grand Rapids, 1975). The work notes the following about the etymology of *oiktirmos:* In classical/secular Greek usage, the word was used to designate "the lamenting or regretting of a person's misfortune or death." Old Testament usage connects the word with *rahamîm* (2:598).
4. Brown notes the following about the etymology of *splagchnon*. In classical/secular Greek usage, the word meant "the inward parts, or entrails (of the sacrificial animal)" and later came to mean the sacrificial meal itself. Because intestines were regarded as the site of natural passions like anger, desire, and love, the word came to metaphorically mean the heart as the seat of feelings and emotions. "The metaphorical meaning have mercy on, feel pity is found only in the writing of Judaism and the New Testament." Only twice does the LXX use *splagchnon* to translate Hebrew words. In Prov. 12:10 it represents *rahamîm* (mercy) and in Prov. 26:22, *beten* (belly). Ibid., 2:599.
5. Brown notes that "the etymological derivation of *pascho* . . . is still not clear." However, in classical/secular Greek usage, the basic meaning is "experiencing something which stems from outside of myself but which affects me, either for good or ill." *Pascho* occurs only twenty-one times in the LXX. It has "no exact equivalent." Ibid., 3:719–20.
6. Brown notes the following about the etymology of *eleeo:* In classical/secular Greek usage, the word was used to designate "the emotion roused by contact with an affliction which comes undeservedly on someone else." Old Testament usage emphasizes the legal concept of covenant relations and God's fidelity. Ibid., 2:594–95.

GLOSSARY

Compassion. Active, personal identification with another human, especially in suffering, with a view to reducing that suffering and bringing *shalom.*

Cult. Religious veneration or worship, whether formal or informal, conscious or subconscious.

Culture. The manifestation of a people's ethos, creed, or sacred belief system. Cultures can change rapidly, slowly, or not at all, depending on the internal dynamics of the culture and shifts in worldview. Ideas spread downward through culture, affecting the way people live and the institutions they build.

Imago Dei. Latin for "in the image of God."

Judeo-Christian theism. The historical worldview of Christendom (the West); theism assumes the existence of a transcendent, infinite-personal God who created the universe—both animate and inanimate, spiritual and physical—as separate from himself but not independent of him. God is both transcendent (outside of his creation) and immanent (present within it). He is everywhere present and involved. The universe is open to God's purpose and intervention. God has revealed himself through special revelation, first through the written Word, the Bible, and then through the living Word, Jesus Christ. At the same time, humans can use their God-given reason to discover truth about God and the universe, because God has revealed himself to all people—the general revelation of creation and of humans being made in his image.

Love. That quality rooted in the nature of God which inclines the lover toward others and shows itself in mercy and compassion.

Materialism. The belief that the soul of man is not a spiritual substance distinct from matter, but that it is the result or effect or the organization of matter in the body (Webster's 1828). This word is used as a synonym for *secularism, secular humanism,* and *atheism.*

Mercy. "Kindness or good will toward the miserable and the afflicted, joined with a desire to help them" (Thayer's *Greek-English Lexicon of the New Testament*).

Moral universe. Acknowledgment of the universe as created by God and as such, an environment in which morality is real and moral choices are significant (as opposed to the atheistic view of the universe as random and inherently amoral).

Poverty. A human condition in which one or more of the fundamental dimensions of life—personal identity, family, community, spirituality, economics, or wisdom—is not functioning.

Secularism. A system that sees the world as ultimately physical and limited, controlled by the blind operations of impersonal natural laws, time, and chance. Secularism renounces spiritual or transcendent reality. It can be summarized by these quotes: "Man is the result of a purposeless and natural process that did not have him in mind" (George Gaylord Simpson), or "Some shrink from the conclusion that the human species was not designed, has no purpose, and is the product of mere mechanical mechanisms—but that seems to be the message of evolution" (Douglas Futuyma). Also known as secular humanism, humanism, or naturalism, this is the increasingly prevalent worldview of the Western world.

Shalom. The opposite of poverty; wholeness of life in every dimension.

Social justice. Justice in the social arena; that state in which vulnerable people (orphans, widows, those in material poverty, immigrants, homeless, et al.) have access to essential human needs (freedom, food, clothing, shelter, justice, etc.) which others take for granted.

State. The central governing authority; nation.

Theism. The belief or system of belief in one God; sees the universe as ultimately personal.

Worldview. A set of assumptions, held consciously or unconsciously, about the basic make-up of the world and how the world works.

SCRIPTURE INDEX

STUDY GUIDE

STUDY GUIDE

This study guide is designed to help you reflect on and apply what you are reading in *Rethinking Social Justice*. It is intended for both individuals and small groups.

HOW TO USE THIS GUIDE

Before you read each section of the book, take time to pray and ask the Holy Spirit to be your teacher. Then read through the study guide for that section; sometimes there are questions to be answered before the reading. You can answer the remaining questions either as you are reading or after you have finished.

Rethinking Social Justice has eight chapters, but this study guide has fifteen sessions to accommodate Sunday schools or similar study programs. You will see a marker in the margin at each point in the book that corresponds with a study guide section. When you come to that marker as you read, stop there and review the study guide for that section.

If you plan to use this study guide in a small-group setting, we suggest a goal of reading and discussing one section each week. Take time to pray and report on the action steps from the previous week's "Do" assignment before discussing new material.

KNOW AND DO: A WORD ABOUT APPLICATION

The ancient Greeks stressed knowing. They wanted to fill the mind with knowledge but had little interest in applying what they learned. The Hebrews, on the other hand, were interested in both knowing and doing the truth. Today, many Christians are more like ancient Greeks than

Hebrews, a sad commentary given that wisdom is the moral application of truth, goodness, and beauty. This study guide will encourage you to have a "Hebrew mind"—to do what you know.

Each session in this study guide has two parts. In the sections marked "Know," you will be challenged with questions to help you reflect on what you have read. The sections marked "Do" will encourage you to put into practice at least one thing you have learned during that week's study.

May God richly bless you as you process the material in *Rethinking Social Justice.*

DARROW L. MILLER
Cofounder of the Disciple Nations Alliance

SESSION 1: INITIAL REFLECTIONS ON YOUR UNDERSTANDING OF SOCIAL JUSTICE

KNOW

1. Before you begin reading this book, take a few minutes to reflect on the following questions.

   a. What are some of the injustices you have seen that have stirred your heart? What kinds of poverty have you witnessed or experienced?

   b. Why do you want to read *Rethinking Social Justice*? What are you hoping to gain from this book?

2. "Never again!" has often been the response to slavery, the Nazi Holocaust, and other such injustices. Yet much personal and institutional evil remains in our world today. The cry of our hearts should be, "What more can I do to stand against today's evil and injustice?"

   a. Take a moment to respond to the cry, "Never again!" Have you ever experienced that emotion related to an injustice? What was the injustice? How did you respond?

   b. What have you been doing to demonstrate God's compassion and justice in your community?

c. What more might God be stirring in your heart?

d. What concerns are holding you back from pursuing the stirrings
    in your heart?

DO

Pray that God would speak to you and teach you about the ancient paths
of justice and compassion as you read this book.

SESSION 2: WHAT IS SOCIAL JUSTICE?

Pre-reading: Please answer these questions *before* you read this section of the book.

1. What motivates you to want to help people who are impoverished?

2. What are you currently doing to fight poverty and injustice?

3. What is your concept of social justice?

KNOW

1. What distinguishes a "sheep church" from a "goat church"?

2. How would you classify your church? Why?

3. According to Timothy Keller, what should our salvation motivate us to do?

4. Why do you think many of our spiritual predecessors failed to respond appropriately to the needs of people around them?

5. What are some of the key insights you gained from the discussion of the definition of social justice?

6. While the term "social justice" is not found in the Bible, the concept is! Based on your reading, how did the phrase and concept develop through church history?

DO

An important sociological maxim says that "before you change a society, you must first change the language." We have given two examples of shifting word definitions that have affected our culture. One relates to what a woman carries in her womb: a "baby" versus a "product of conception." The second relates to the changing definition of social justice.

1. Discuss with a friend or small group the meaning and implications of this sociological maxim.

2. Discuss how the language shifts surrounding pregnancy and social justice are bringing real changes to society.

3. Identify another language shift you are witnessing in your society. Discuss the implications of that shift.

SESSION 3: EQUALITY VERSUS EQUITY

Pre-reading: Please answer these questions *before* you read this section of the book.

1. What is your concept of equality?

2. In what ways are people equal?

3. In what ways are people distinct from each other?

4. Why do you think there is so much heat around discussions of social justice?

KNOW

1. Describe the difference between equality and equity.

2. When can treating everybody the same be unjust?

3. What insight does C. S. Lewis bring to this question?

4. Describe, in your own words, the implications of the "Four P" diagram (page 32).

5. Explain how the way we define a problem will determine how we solve the problem.

6. Identify and describe the three types of evil.

7. How did Dietrich Bonhoeffer respond to the growing evil in Germany during the Third Reich? What do you think it cost him in the short run? What did it cost him in the long run?

DO

1. Describe, in your own words, the three stages of Bonhoeffer's call to the church to help the Jews during World War II.

2. What comparable process could apply to the church today? How can you get involved?

SESSION 4: THE UNIVERSE, ECONOMICS, AND MORALITY

KNOW

1. What is meant by

    a. an open system?

    b. a closed system?

2. Why is this distinction important in a discussion of social justice?

3. Similarly, what is the difference between a *zero-sum* and a *positive-sum* economic system in relationship to creating wealth and solving the problems associated with poverty?

4. Briefly describe some characteristics of people in each of the four quadrants on page 36.

    a. Upper right

    b. Lower left

c.   Lower right

d.   Upper left

DO

1.   Look again at the diagram on page 36. Which of the four quadrants best represents what your life has exemplified? (Be honest!) Has reading this section changed your thinking in any way?

2.   Look for examples of each of these worldviews (open system versus closed system, moral versus amoral) in approaches to poverty and injustice. (For instance, find three organizations and examine them in light of these worldviews.)

SESSION 5: THE TEST OF TRUTH

KNOW

1. What is one of the tests for success or failure in poverty-alleviating programs?

2. What point does economic philosopher Michael Novak make concerning US poverty-fighting programs?

3. What do most redistribution programs end up doing?

4. Steve Chapman, a writer for the *Chicago Tribune*, in commenting on statist-redistributionist models of poverty reduction, says that "even communists eventually have to make peace with reality." What does he mean?

5. In what dimension of life is the root of injustice found? Please explain.

6. Why has so much Christian activity in Haiti—from preaching the gospel to establishing churches, Bible schools, and seminaries, to relief and development work—had so little impact? What conclusions can be drawn from this observation?

7. Describe how the spiritual realm impacts the physical realm through culture.

8. What does it mean that ordinary Christians need to learn to *think theologically* about their work? How can you begin to do this in your work?

DO

1. As Christians we should spend more time extending justice to others and less time demanding justice for ourselves. List five ways you tend to blame others for your circumstances or expect people to treat you more justly.

2. Identify someone in your school, workplace, or community who is seen as an outcast. How might you befriend them?

3. The next time you see someone treated as socially "invisible," how might you treat him or her with dignity?

SESSION 6: THE DEMISE OF SOCIAL JUSTICE

Pre-reading: Please answer this question *before* you read this section of the book.

What is the standard by which you measure someone's compassion?

KNOW

1. What synonyms for *compassion* can you think of?

2. According to Dr. Robert Ellis Thompson, how should we measure compassion?

3. What is your response to Thompson?

4. The sociological maxim states that "you must change language before changing culture."

    a. Explain in your own words what this means.

b.   How has the word *compassion* changed?

c.   What other words are shifting in your culture?

5.   What is the root of (biblical) compassion?

6.   Describe how Jesus treated compassion as a verb rather than a noun.

7.   According to Gary Haugen, what should be the relationship between compassion and action?

8.   Fill in the blanks from page 52: _____'s nature is compassion. He acts compassionately and expects _____ to _____. True social justice is _____ _____ and _____. To commiserate is to be in such a _____ with the person so as to _____.

9.   How did Zachary Macaulay identify with African slaves?

10. Imagine if you had done what Macaulay did. What risks would you have faced?

11. As Western culture has shifted from the Judeo-Christian world-view of the Bible to an atheist-materialist worldview, our definition of compassion has shifted. Look at the table on page 55. How have things changed? What is your response to that change?

DO

1. Take time to reflect on Count Zinzendorf's confrontation with the words of Christ: "This have I done for you—What will you do for me?" On a heart level, how would you respond to the question?

2. Identify an individual in your extended community who is in need of compassion.

    a. How could you identify with him/her?

    b. How could you walk with him/her?

    c. What one thing will you do in the next week to be neighborly to this person?

SESSION 7: THE ROOT OF POVERTY

KNOW

1. In your own words, share how the "Four P" diagram on page 32 explains that ideas have consequences.

2. The history and health of a nation turn on ideas. Throughout history, certain people have brought about ideological shifts. Such is the case in the area of compassion, as the following examples indicate.

    a. The founders of the Salvation Army, William and Catherine Booth, held one view of the root of poverty, while their fellow Englishman Charles Booth held another. What was the distinction between these two views?

    b. In the United States, a similar debate about approaches to poverty was taking place between two newspaper publishers, Henry Raymond and Horace Greeley. What characterized the distinction between their approaches?

    c. Given our current understanding of social justice, which side won each debate? Why is this significant?

3. How did the great Russian novelist Leo Tolstoy define the root of our

problem? What does this have to do with poverty and compassion?

4. As worldviews have shifted, so has language, leading to a change in the policies and programs of poverty alleviation.

    a. Describe how Michael Harrington's concept of "structural poverty" contributed to these changes.

    b. Describe how Fernando Cardosa's "dependency theory" contributed to these changes.

5. How do these concepts actually hinder people who are poor from employing the tools God has given them to flourish?

6. How have these language shifts infected your thinking and impacted your actions?

DO

Reflect on the consequences ideas have on poverty and compassion. How have you been influenced (consciously or subconsciously) by your attitudes toward and engagement with the world of poverty? How might you need to retrain your mind to think about poverty from a biblical perspective?

SESSION 8: HOW A CORRUPTED WORSHIP ADULTERATED OUR COMPASSION

KNOW

1. We have touched on the concept of "cult" as a synonym for "worship" (see pages 32, 44, and 63). Describe in your own words the relationship between worship (*cult*) and the creation of *culture* or the kinds of nations we build.

2. There are three distinct models of compassion. Describe the characteristics of each model and give an example of each.

   a. Judeo-Christian social teaching

   b. Social Darwinism

   c. Social Universalism

3. According to Ken Wytsma, what is the significance of the Hebrew word *tsedek*?

4. What are the differences between passive and proactive social Darwinism?

5. What have been some instances of proactive social Darwinism in history?

6. Where do you see proactive social Darwinism today?

7. This shift in worldview has affected our view and practice of compassion in at least five dimensions of society. List and explain the five areas.

8. How has the shift from personal relationships to financial transactions impacted the way we think about and act toward God's mission to disciple nations?

DO

Develop a short teaching or informal facilitation curriculum on either the three distinct models of compassion or the demise of compassion. Share this with a friend or small-group Bible study.

SESSION 9: THE OXYMORON OF ATHEISTIC COMPASSION

KNOW

1. Why does atheism provide no basis for compassion and social justice?

2. Why, in spite of the above, are many atheists actually compassionate?

3. What does Gertrude Himmelfarb mean by "telescopic philanthropy"?

4. How did the different *social philosophies* of Max Weber and Karl Marx work out in the real world?

5. How did the different *economic philosophies* of Adam Smith and Thomas Malthus work out in the real world?

6. What three significant shifts in economic theory/practice took place as a result of the Malthusian/materialist worldview?

DO

1. Reflect on the example of the opportunities and wealth that Steve Jobs and Steve Wozniak created from an idea. Can you cite another example in which someone created wealth with limited material resources?

2. Examine your own life.

   a. How do you exhibit habits that support the creation of wealth?

   b. In what ways are you a "taker" or consumer of wealth?

3. Identify one area in your life where you can be . . .

   a. more creative.

   b. more giving.

SESSION 10: RADICAL SOCIAL JUSTICE: THE BIBLICAL IMPERATIVE

KNOW

1. Why does it matter that compassion (aka social justice) is rooted in the heart of God?

2. Why has our understanding and practice of social justice eroded?

3. What three key ideas about the biblical words for compassion do we get from a study of Scripture?

4. The first Old Testament word we studied is *chamal,* "to treat with tenderness."

    a. What have you learned (on a heart level) in studying this concept?

    b. Identify someone you know who has manifested *chamal.* How did he or she display this quality?

c. Describe one time you treated someone with tenderness. What was the result for the person and for you?

5. What have you learned (on a heart level) from studying the Hebrew term *rahamîm* and its family of related words?

6. What is the archetype of a mother's and father's compassion? What is significant about this?

7. We studied the Greek word *oiktirmos,* "mercy." Identify someone you know who has manifested mercy. How did he or she display this quality?

8. We looked at an Old Testament–New Testament couplet, the Hebrew *chesed* and the Greek *eleos,* both of which mean "loving-kindness."

a. What have you learned (on a heart level) in studying this concept?

b. Identify someone you know who has manifested loving-kindness. How did he or she display this quality?

c.   To whom in your life could you show more loving-kindness? Be
     specific.

DO

1.   Words reflect our worldviews and impact our actions. My (Darrow's)
     own life has powerfully changed since I understood the importance
     of affirming biblical *virtues* rather than simply recognizing *values*, of
     embracing *truth* rather than mere *beliefs*, of acknowledging a *baby*
     rather than a *fetus* or a *product of conception*. Identify one word you are
     in the habit of using that may not reflect a biblical worldview. How
     will you plan to abandon that word? What biblical vocabulary can
     you use to replace it?

2.   Pick one of the people you identified as manifesting one of these
     characteristics of compassion. Following his or her example, do
     something similar for someone or for a cause of justice during the
     next week. In other words, "Go and do likewise!" State specifically
     what you will do.

SESSION 11: A COMPASSIONATE CHRIST

KNOW

1. The first New Testament word we studied is *splagchnizomai*, "compassion," as characterized by Christ.

    a. What have you learned (on a heart level) in studying this concept?

    b. Identify someone you know who has manifested the compassion of Christ. How did he or she display this quality?

2. The second New Testament word is *pascho*, "suffering," as of the suffering Servant, Christ.

    a. What have you learned (on a heart level) in studying this concept?

    b. Christ suffered not to set us free *from* suffering but to set us free *for* suffering. What does this mean? How does it apply to you?

    c. Identify someone you know who has manifested being a "suffering servant." How did he or she display this quality?

3. What three dimensions of Christ's suffering were mentioned? What does each mean for you?

4. William Barclay, in his commentary on the Lord's Prayer and the Beatitudes, describes the culture of cruelty during Christ's day. Describe some of the cruelty you see in your own community and culture.

5. What stands out to you in the Walter Brueggemann quote? What do you agree or disagree with?

DO

1. The pursuit of justice often exacts a cost. What cost have you paid in the past for seeking justice?

2. What price might you have to pay in the future as you contemplate engaging more in social justice?

SESSION 12: PRINCIPLES OF COMPASSION, PART 1

KNOW

1. What is the relationship between worldview and development?

2. According to Timothy Keller, what is the inescapable conclusion of living according to the Bible?

3. Why is it a Christian concern to address physical ills such as poverty and hunger?

4. What is *affiliation*? How is it critical to the practice of social justice?

5. What is *bonding*? How is it critical to the practice of social justice?

6. What is *categorization*? How is it critical to the practice of social justice?

DO

1. Holiness has a public component as well as a personal one. What can you do to call your church or small group to work for public holiness?

2. Examine the practices of social justice in which you have engaged. Have those practices involved any of these principles? If so, which ones?

3. Describe how you can apply one of these principles in an area of poverty for which you have a heart.

SESSION 13: PRINCIPLES OF COMPASSION, PART 2

KNOW

1. What is *discernment*? How is it critical to the practice of social justice?

2. What questions should we honestly ask ourselves before beginning a charitable activity?

3. What is *employment*? How is it critical to the practice of social justice?

4. What is *freedom*? How is it critical to the practice of social justice?

5. Why is *God* one of the principles of compassion? Briefly summarize the argument of this section.

6. List Gary Haugen's four truths about the character of God that lead to social justice.

7. What does it mean that "generosity of compassion is not measured by a number of dollars but by nobility of character, quality of time, and value of service"? How do you react to this statement?

8. What stands out to you in Emperor Julian's statement?

DO

1. Given the need for discernment in our engagement in social justice, take a few minutes to reflect on your true motivations for helping the poor and fighting for social justice. Ask someone who knows you well (a close friend, spouse, parent) to tell you what they think your motivations are. Don't be afraid of honesty! It will help you serve the Lord better.

2. As we come to the end of our journey of rethinking social justice, review some of the principles you have learned and describe how you will apply these in your ministry of compassion. List at least five.

SESSION 14: COMPASSION IN ACTION

KNOW

1. After reading all these stories, identify the two that most impressed you. For each one answer the following.

    a.   Story 1:

        What most impressed you about this story?

        What principles of compassion can you glean from this story?

    b.   Story 2:

        What most impressed you about this story?

        What principles of compassion can you glean from this story?

2. Identify a story from your own experience, something that you have been personally involved with or observed, which touches on compassion.

a.   Describe the story.

b.   What most impressed you?

c.   What principles of compassion can you glean from this story?

DO

1.   With a group of friends, pray about a need in your community that God might want you to address.*

2.   Identify the need.

3.   What are God's intentions? That is, what would things look like if the problem were gone?

4.   What Scripture reinforces the solution to the problem?

* For much more on this, read Bob Moffitt's *If Jesus Were Mayor: How Your Local Church Can Transform Your Community* (Harvest, 2006).

5.   What will you call your project?

6.   How will you engage with the people whose problem you seek to address? How will they become a part of the solution so that they are empowered to solve their own problems?

SESSION 15: POPE FRANCIS AND SOCIAL JUSTICE

KNOW

1. Pope Francis uses the phrase "ethical mobilization" when he speaks of social justice.

   a. What does he mean by this?

   b. Why is this important to the discussion of social justice?

2. How does the naturalistic framework of modern society influence and limit the terms of the discussion of social justice?

3. What are the three basic forms of evil in the world? How are they the same and how is each unique?

4. What is "throwaway culture"? Where do you see this culture in your own community? Where do you see it in your own life?

5. Pope Francis speaks of the "culture of death." What is this culture, and how does it lead to injustice in a society?

6. How is "the gaze of Jesus" significant for dealing with issues of social justice?

7. Why does Pope Francis root social justice in God-given human dignity?

8. Why is "throwing money" not the solution to problems of poverty and injustice?

DO

1. Return to session 1 of the study guide and think about your original goal for reading the book. To what extent was your goal met?

2. Make a list of the most important things you have learned from this book.

3. Identify one thing you have not done before that you will seek to apply in your life in the years ahead.

ACKNOWLEDGMENTS

I want to thank our friend John Stonestreet of BreakPoint and Summit Ministries, who challenged the DNA to write on the subject of social justice. Without that prompting, this project might never have seen the light of day.

I am grateful for those generations who have come before and modeled for us the heart of the Christian life: to seek justice, love mercy, and walk humbly before God.

Thank you to those whose writings on compassion have been a challenge and encouragement. These include historian and moral philosopher Gertrude Himmelfarb and our good friend Marvin Olasky, editor-in-chief of *World* magazine. Marvin's work *The Tragedy of American Compassion* was instrumental in shaping Scott Allen's and my thinking in the 1990s as we were exploring the relationship between worldview and issues of poverty and compassion. Thank you, Marvin.

Thanks to my friend and colaborer Dr. Bob Moffitt and the global team at Harvest Foundation, who have taught and modeled compassion through Seed Projects and Disciplines of Love.

Thanks to my colaborers and partner organizations in the Disciple Nations Alliance whose lives and ministries have been an encouragement and challenge to us!

Thank you to our friend and colaborer Viviana Velie, our Spanish publisher. Thank you for your vision to see the nations of the Spanish-speaking world transformed by the gospel of the kingdom and for pushing us to write more books that contribute to that end.

Thanks as well to the team at YWAM Publishing. For over fifteen years you have partnered with us to get the messages of the Disciple Nations Alliance to the larger world. Thanks to publisher Tom Bragg for your vision for these messages. Thanks to our longtime friend and project director Warren Walsh, who has labored over the years to get our books into print. And thanks to Ryan Davis, our editor, whose work on structure, flow, and language always makes our books far better reads.

A special thanks to Mary Kaech, who helped with the study guide and gave feedback on the larger project.

What a pleasure it is to work with friends Scott Allen and Gary Brumbelow. Thank you both for our times of thinking and reflecting together and for your faithful application of the writing gifts God has bestowed. This project is every bit as much yours as it has been mine.

Thanks as well to Mary Kaech and Shawn Carson for their research help.

I am indebted to all of these friends for their contributions, but any errors in the book are wholly mine.

Above all, I am grateful to our Lord and Savior, Jesus Christ, who is Compassion and whose compassion has so dramatically touched my life.

ABOUT THE AUTHORS

DARROW L. MILLER

For over thirty years, Darrow L. Miller has been a popular speaker on Christianity and culture, apologetics, worldview, poverty, and the dignity of women. He has traveled and lectured in more than one hundred countries, and his articles, books, and publications have been translated into twenty languages.

Darrow has a master's degree in higher and adult education and has pursued graduate studies in philosophy, theology, Christian apologetics, biblical studies, and missions. He and his wife, Marilyn, studied at the Institute for Holy Land Studies in Jerusalem and studied and worked with Francis and Edith Schaeffer at L'Abri Fellowship in Switzerland from 1969 to 1971.

For twenty-seven years, Darrow served as a vice president of Food for the Hungry International (FHI) in the areas of recruiting, staff development, and the creation of curriculum in worldview and development. While at FHI, he cofounded the Disciple Nations Alliance (DNA) with Dr. Bob Moffitt and Scott Allen. The DNA is a nonprofit organization seeking to spread a school of thought—a virus, if you will—through training, publishing, and mentoring. Our vision is to see the global church rise to her full potential as God's instrument for the healing, blessing, and transforming of the nations. The global DNA network comprises like-minded organizations and people in over sixty countries who are "equipping the church to transform the world."

Darrow and his wife live in Blue Ridge, Arizona. They have four children and fourteen grandchildren.

SCOTT ALLEN

After graduating with his bachelor's degree in history from Willamette University in Salem, Oregon, in 1988, Scott joined Food for the Hungry International, where he served until 2007, holding positions in both Japan and the United States in areas of human resources, staff training, and program management. Along with Darrow Miller and Bob Moffitt, Scott helped launch the Disciple Nations Alliance. He has authored and cowritten a number of books, including the Kingdom Lifestyle Bible Study Series, a set of four studies containing *Beyond the Sacred-Secular Divide: A Call to Wholistic Life and Ministry*. His most recent book is titled *As the Family Goes, So Goes the Nation*. Scott lives with his wife, Kim, and their five children in Phoenix, Arizona.

GARY BRUMBELOW

Gary served as a cross-cultural missionary among Canada's First Nations peoples for eight years before working in missionary administration for twenty-four years, including fourteen years as executive director of Inter-Act Ministries. In 2010, he joined the Disciple Nations Alliance, where he manages the *Darrow Miller and Friends* blog and serves as a cowriter and editor: sometimes by converting ideas into prose, sometimes by simply burnishing good writing. He has an MA in communication from Wheaton College and a graduate diploma from Western Seminary. His writing has appeared in *PULSE*, *Evangelical Missions Quarterly*, and other publications. He and his wife, Valerie, have two married sons and nine grandchildren. They live in Boring, Oregon.

Disciple
Nations
Alliance

Equipping the Church to Transform the World

The Disciple Nations Alliance is a global network of individuals, churches, and organizations with a common vision: *to see the global church rise to her full potential as God's instrument for the healing, blessing, and transforming of the nations.*

The Disciple Nations Alliance was founded in 1997 through a partnership between Food for the Hungry (www.fh.org) and Harvest (www. harvestfoundation.org). Our mission is to influence the *paradigm* and *practice* of local churches around the world, helping them to recognize and abandon false beliefs and embrace a robust biblical worldview—bringing truth, justice, and beauty into every sphere of society—and to demonstrate Christ's love in practical ways, addressing the brokenness in communities and nations beginning with their own resources.

For more information about the Disciple Nations Alliance and to find a host of resources, curricula, books, study materials, and application tools, please visit our website:

www.disciplenations.org
E-mail: info@disciplenations.org